HO
THE REAL ME

ROCK:
THE REAL ME

HOCK:
THE REAL ME

As told to
NEIL BARKER

Scratching Shed Publishing Ltd

Cover photography: © Paul McCarthy Photography.

Interior photography: All images from the personal
collection of Gareth Hock or courtesy of
www.rlphotos.com unless otherwise stated

A catalogue record for this book is available from the
British Library.

Typeset in Warnock Pro Semi Bold and Palatino
Printed and bound in the United Kingdom by
Charlesworth Press, Flanshaw Way, Flanshaw Lane,
Wakefield, WF2 9LP

For Danielle,
Wade, Lucas, Billy and Heidi

Contents

66 My temper and
hot-headedness
has always let
me down. Like most
people, I have done
a lot of things that I
regret..." -
Gareth Hock

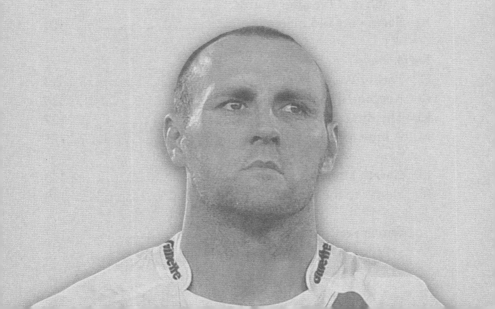

Acknowledgements
Neil Barker

Thanks go to the following people and parties for their help and support in the preparation of Gareth's book.

To my own wife Janice, son Tom and daughter Hannah for their plentiful enthusiasm and encouragement. Cheers you guys. Also to Neil Leigh, Mike Latham, Mick Hannan, Maurice Lindsay and Shaun Wane – all fine men – who were given an early insight into the core of the story. Their favourable comments on social media and in person were greatly appreciated.

Immense gratitude goes to publishers Scratching Shed, for supporting the project and being willing to turn an idea into print.

An initial approach for help in typing the copy saw the administrative skills of Karen Patten and Christine Swann, a lifelong Wigan fan, play key roles in helping it take shape.

Christine's professionalism, not only on the keyboard but also in expertly proof-reading the content, was invaluable.

Most importantly, I must express my appreciation for the honesty and integrity of Gareth and his partner Danielle themselves, ensuring that the time spent in their company resulted in the truly fascinating account of a never less than eventful professional rugby league career you now have in your possession.

Neil Barker, October 2015

Foreword

Adrian Morley

The first time I heard the name 'Gaz' Hock I was playing with Sydney City Roosters in Australia. It was during a phonecall back home to my old teammate and friend, the late Leeds, Bradford, Wakefield and Wigan player, Terry Newton.

He says: 'You've got to see this young lad Hock play. He reminds me of you when you were coming through at Leeds.' I made a mental note of the name.

The first time I got to play with him was at the end of my time there on the Great Britain tour of Australia in 2006. I was immediately impressed, firstly with him as a player but, more importantly, as a lad.

On the field, he was extremely aggressive. Up front, when you get one of your fellow forwards putting it about, it makes your job a lot easier. But Gaz wasn't just an enforcer, he had a real rugby brain and showed some quality touches with the ball in hand.

Growing up, Gaz was one of Tez Newton's best mates, as I was. Knowing the kind of lads that Terry knocked about with I was confident we'd get on. I was proven right. We got on great. In fact, out of all the tours I've been on with England or Great Britain, alongside Gaz and Tez amongst others, that tour was easily the most enjoyable.

I got to play with him at domestic level too in 2014, at my hometown club Salford Red Devils. It didn't work out for him there, which was a massive shame. The Salford faithful never got to see Gaz Hock at his best. On his day he was virtually unstoppable.

Gaz has had many ups and downs in both his career and his private life. He is the classic player that opposing teams' fans love to boo and jeer.

Think what you want about him, though, what you can't ever do is question his talent and love for rugby league.

Gaz, it has been a pleasure to play with you and against you. I'm proud to call you a mate.

Adrian Morley, September 2015

Introduction

Neil Barker

Born to play rugby league for his beloved Wigan, it has been claimed Gareth Hock had the potential to have been one of the best players in the world.

Hock had seemingly everything in his locker.

He definitely should have been high up there brushing shoulders with the game's all-time greats.

Some of the biggest personalities in the Wigan club's history watched and were appreciative of the emergence of a lion-hearted local hero who combined God-given sublime skill with raw-boned aggression.

Add to that a powerhouse determination and burning desire to emulate his hero, Andy Farrell, and it should have been the perfect combination.

Yet it never quite turned out that way.

Throughout a rollercoaster career, Hock has very often

Hock: The Real Me

Complex character:
Gareth Hock –
revitalised at Leigh

self-destructed and been easily led. There have been times when he has been his own worst enemy.

He has let himself down on and off the field.

He has, however, been a handful for everyone from the local police to the star-studded Australian national team. And he is still a hard man on a mission, man enough to admit to his failings and seek to put them right.

He knows he has made mistakes along the way.

He has thrown many punches, diced with death even, scored tries, shed tears and shown varying sides to his nature.

Regarded as a complex character by many in the sport, some genuine insight into the real Gareth Hock and what makes him tick will hopefully unfold in the pages ahead.

It is a remarkable rags to riches story – a tale dogged by the pitfalls and perils that line life's highway.

It is also a glowing testimony to the character and staying power of the man at its heart.

Gareth Hock has had to climb from the canvas on many occasions. He has survived a few standing counts but is still doing what he does best and that's playing rugby league.

Respected and feared by rivals, Hock keeps himself to himself. Yet he has always needed people to talk to, from whom he might gain help and guidance – people he can trust.

In return, a happy Hock does what he does best by playing well. He likes to do his talking on the field.

Off it, he has no edge to him.

Gareth approached me early in 2015 to see if I would help him to write his book. We go back a long way. He said I am the only reporter he has ever trusted and got on with, a nice thing to hear indeed.

For my part, I have always followed his career with interest – rated him highly – and like the fact that he is a fellow Wiganer with a fascinating story to tell.

Hock: The Real Me

Sitting down and simply chatting with Gareth was eye-opening. The memories soon came flooding back.

Players, games and some sticky situations came to light that had been stored away in the memory vault.

We laughed, we cross-examined one another and we talked at length. I got to know the real Gareth Hock.

I thought I already knew a man who spent so much of his time in the headlines but, like so many others, it turned out that I was badly mistaken.

I greatly admire the lad for his honesty in all of this.

Hock has done many foolish things, but he has also done a great deal of good and brought pleasure to many.

Now a happily settled and caring family man, he is among a dying breed of real rugby league characters.

I have seen him turn in some brilliant world class performances. I have also seen the red mist come down.

I have seen his disappointments and witnessed him at his lowest level.

Whatever I have seen though, I have always made time to speak to Gareth.

This was so very important.

To have been involved with the project has been both an honour and a thrill.

Hock is a fine player and a good man who would part with his last penny and help anyone.

The real Gareth Hock is about to stand up and be counted.

Neil Barker, Wigan, 2015

HOCK
THE REAL ME

Drugs almost killed me...

1

God only knows how I have never done time. I have been a bad 'un as we say in Wigan and had my share of drugs. Rugby league has however been my salvation; it has kept my head above water, just.

Nor have I ever known my real father. I changed my name as a 12-year-old from Gareth Charnock to Gareth Hock when my folks split up.

I was banned from driving aged 16.

We 'borrowed' a Ford Fiesta and went for a drive in Marsh Green, but the police nabbed us. The dad of my future Wigan teammate Paul Johnson ran after me with his dog and caught me. My card was marked. I wasn't even driving but they threw the book at us and we were punished hard.

By then, I had already signed for Wigan. I did that when I was 11 and got an £11,000 package, proud as punch.

Hock: The Real Me

But school was not for me. I hated it, wagged it and lived for rugby league. I was hardly ever there and had regular run-ins with the local Bobbies. They knew who I was alright.

Along with a driving ban, 16 was also the age when I first got into drugs.

It all started with an ecstasy tablet given to me by a mate on a Friday night out in Wigan. We were in the Turnkey, I took it and was instantly buzzing – fucking magic I thought!

I needed more and got more. I became reliant on them and was soon hooked.

I lived for the weekends in Wigan Pier with my mates Terry Caddick, Mark Roberts, Dave Watson and Phil Higham. Us Norley lads are still close. In hindsight I wouldn't do drugs again, but I was young, reckless and crazy and needed my fix. They almost killed me.

In 2009, my whole world crumbled to pieces, due to what they call the 'devil's dandruff'.

I was living in Ashton, at the time. It was a warm June night, my mates were around for a barbeque and the beer was flowing. My form for Wigan was good but we were partying hard and I just thought: 'Fuck it; give me some of that cocaine.' It was being passed around like toffee.

What a dick head, but I've always been easily led and willpower has never been a strength. What I did was utter madness.

We were due to play Salford at the weekend and, as usual, one player from each side was selected after that match for a random drugs test. I was one of them.

I waited until around 11pm before peeing in a bottle, hoping the cocaine wouldn't show.

I chanced it, that's the gambler in me.

I then flew to Paris the day after with the England team,

hearing nothing for two weeks and assuming that I was in the clear. One day, though, my Wigan teammates Terry Newton and Terry O'Connor took me to one side, saying that they'd heard on the QT that I was in big bother.

It still didn't stop me going on holiday to Ibiza and I turned my phone off while I was away.

Dr Chris Brookes, the Wigan doctor, still hadn't heard anything about the test when I left.

But on my return the Rugby Football League rang me on my mobile. I thought it was some of the Wigan lads taking the piss so just said: 'Fuck off, pull the other one,' and ended the call.

But then Brian Noble, at that time the Wigan coach, got through to tell me that a positive test had been confirmed.

My heart sank. I was instantly gutted.

There and then, my world fell apart. I went to the club, picked up my gear and faced up to two years of hell – the amount of time I ended up being banned for after a second 'B' sample also returned positive for benzoylecgonine, the main metabolite of cocaine.

In August, the final mandatory decision was handed down and I didn't bother to appeal it.

No rugby meant I was depressed and suicidal. I went and got pissed there and then. Before going out on the drink my Mum saw me and sensed I was in big trouble.

Wigan's new owner, Ian Lenagan, said the club would be standing by me and they did. I was on a good contract, but Wigan made me sign an additional agreement stating I would not sign for any other club on my return.

I had six months off and labouring on building sites and the like introduced me to the real world.

Even so, Wigan were paying me £35,000 per year while I was out. And the club also introduced me to Lee Robinson,

Failing the test: It was after this match with Salford in 2009 that I landed my two-year ban

a personal trainer who put me through hell as I got my life and fitness on track. Lee remains a great mate – we went into the schools coaching and immediately hit it off. He threw me a lifeline and I am still indebted to him for that.

Drugs though is not a road to go down. It is a killer.

Keiron McNamara was another good mate who is sadly no longer with us.

He had the misfortune to die due to drugs and I ended up carrying his coffin.

Keiron was from Beech Hill, one of the best. I learned of his death when I was in South Africa, pre-season training with Salford. Coming to terms with his death was bloody hard.

By then, I had also lost another 'brother': Terry Newton.

The enforced time out put my life into perspective and I quickly came to realise what an idiot I had been.

I'd had the world at my feet – I was playing for Wigan, the best known rugby league club in the world, and had balls-ed it up good style.

I had self-destructed, an additional habit on top of all the drugs, drink and crazy times.

I remember looking at myself in the mirror one morning and saying: 'For fuck's sake, this has got to stop.' But for some unknown reason it couldn't.

Things kept on going from bad to worse.

Born to run: I actually began my rugby league career as a typical skinny halfback

It's a hard knock life...

2

Like I say, I don't know who my real father is. I have never met him and I probably never will. My mum, Kim, brought the family up on Severn Drive in the tough district of Norley Hall, where the dogs like biting postmens' shins.

I have two sisters, Kirsty – who went on to marry the current Widnes Vikings' captain and former Wigan and Huddersfield stand-off, Kevin Brown – and Cody.

I love both my sisters to bits and my mum is a strong and special woman with a big heart.

Damian Hock, her partner, is the man I have always classed as 'Dad'. He is a former Mr Wigan who was a tough-tackling loose forward with local amateur side St Cuthbert's. I have always had a good supportive family who have always provided for me.

I have played for Cuth's and Wigan St Judes myself

and – occasionally – went to Thomas More High School. Present day Wigan coach Shaun Wane, another hard lad who I have always respected, was from the same estate.

Friday nights often ended up with me scrapping and in a bit of bother.

Kelly Ryder, a Marsh Green girl, was my first real serious girlfriend. We met at 15 and I was with her for two years. We still keep in touch.

Being dyslexic never helped me at school. I struggled to read and write for a long time.

I soon got in with the wrong crowd too, bunking off, but always made time for the rugby team. Maurice Lindsay, the former Wigan chairman, used to say that I was born to play rugby – and he was right.

Growing up, I played halfback at first and was a typical one at that. A bit frail physically, I was always in mischief, yet my family were always there for me.

Years later, Damian was absolutely gutted when I landed my two-year drugs ban. He is a massive Wigan fan and I idolised Andrew Farrell myself – what a player!

I wanted to be just like him.

Jack Robinson and Derek Standish first signed me for Wigan from St Judes in 1994, when I was just 11. I went down to Central Park, signed on the dotted line and began counting down the days until I could play as a professional.

Huddersfield scrum-half Luke Robinson signed at the same time and he also had to wait.

After that it was a case of working my way up through the club's tried and tested scholarship and academy systems, where Wigan threequarter and halfback of the late 1980s, Ged Byrne, was my first academy coach.

I left school the first chance I got – hardly surprising – never sat exams and don't have an academic qualification to

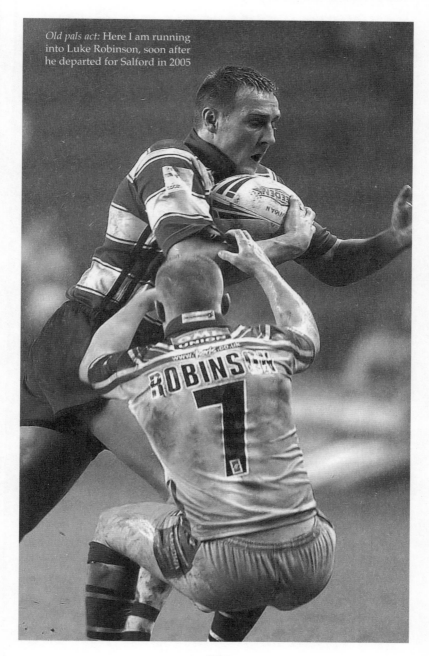

Old pals act: Here I am running into Luke Robinson, soon after he departed for Salford in 2005

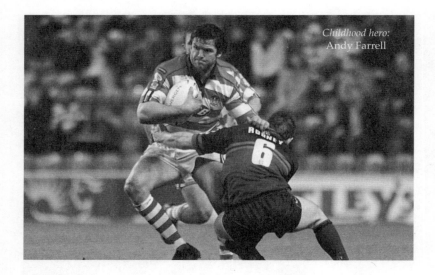

Childhood hero:
Andy Farrell

my name, preferring to join Ged on his window cleaning round in Aspull instead.

We had a good crack and he put a few quid my way.

Playing for the junior teams at Wigan was a massive honour. I was hell bent on making the grade and one day running out alongside Farrell. Nothing was going to stop me.

My teammates in those days included Mark Roberts, Sean O'Loughlin, Billy Joe Edwards, Gary Winstanley, Lee Ford and Luke Robinson, of course.

All good players, great lads and all proud to play for Wigan.

Star maker was Brian Foley, head of the scholarship scheme, who was always there to keep an eye on me because of my reputation. Later, he described me as 'a streetwise lad' who it could have gone either way for.

Talking to the papers in 2003, he called me 'a character' and explained: 'Part of the scholarship scheme is to give lads guidance off the field as well as on it and I remember sitting him down for a chat, saying that we should start again. A

Early teammate:
Sean O'Loughlin

couple of weeks later I was reading out the register at Central Park and when I said "Gareth Charnock", there was no answer. When I asked him what was going on, he told me he was making a fresh start as Gareth Hock.'

I have so much time for Brian, a great man and a tough task master. You didn't piss about with Brian. He was a military man and apparently a bare knuckle boxer.

He told me to come back as a new man and I did!

Brian simply laughed – we got on brilliantly.

While in the junior ranks I also played Town Team and knew that rugby league was where my money was going to come from, and how it would keep me out of prison.

Mixing drugs with playing though was such a massive risk to all of that.

Why I did it I just don't know, other than that it gave me a buzz. And eventually I would lose big time, on that terrible night when I peed in a bottle after we played Salford.

Hometown boy: Running out with Wigan in 2004 – the club I was always destined to play for

The Wigan years...

3

I have already mentioned former Wigan chairman Maurice Lindsay – they used to call him Mr Wigan.

I will always have the utmost respect for Maurice.

He talked me up and claimed I had the talent to be really big in the game – one of the best.

If only, eh?

I went on to gain international honours at academy level and Warrington too had watched me as a schoolboy.

When you were raised on the tough streets of Norley Hall, though, you only ever want to play for one club and you bleed cherry blood.

Ged Byrne gave me my chance in the juniors and I didn't let anyone down.

Kiwi Frank Endacott brought me onto the fringes of the first team and I was on my way, but it was an Aussie, Stuart

Raper, who gave me my debut in 2003. It came against Doncaster in that year's Challenge Cup, when I scored a couple of tries from the bench.

Maurice always saw me as a rough diamond. He knew what I could do on the field and he has always looked out for me. When in 2009 I got my drugs ban, it was Maurice who organised for the *News of the World* to print my warts and all story on what I had done.

They pushed me to the limit to lift the lid on other big name stars who were also drug users and top players. I didn't bite and just pocketed the five-figure fee.

I was honest and up front in the article.

There will always be players who do what I did – taking drugs and playing. It is still going on today. It's common and it will continue, such is society.

The more you do it and the longer this goes on without you getting caught, then the bigger the buzz it gives you.

Players will chance it until they are caught – which is exactly what happened to me.

I only ever did drugs at weekends, after games and when we went up town. I would spend hundreds of pounds getting my hands on top brand cocaine.

I had to have it.

The problem starts when you are young. I feel your background can greatly influence the need to do it.

It did with me because I was familiar with this vice at an early age and soon fell into the trap.

It took hold and there was no escape.

Why do players do recreational drugs? Well, it helps them get away from the pressures. You use it as an escape valve away from rugby.

Lads are doing it as we speak. It's rife, it's wrong and it's the road to self-ruination. Thankfully, I eventually realised this. You become addicted and it can kill you if you're not careful.

Your head is all over the place and I was treading a fine line yet still playing top-flight rugby. How the fuck I did it, Christ only knows.

I can remember that Wigan debut as if it was yesterday. Two tries after coming on for the injured Mick Cassidy and I was a first team regular from that point on. It was a lucky break for me – if not for Mick!

I had only ever wanted to be a one-club man.

'Happy' Frank Endacott was a top bloke and I was sorry to see him go when he left the club in 2001. But I also got on fine with Raper, his replacement, and played under the late Mike Gregory in 2003-2004 too. Mike was the tops and I played for him at international academy level as well.

In fact I built up a lot of experience in youth rugby, which probably helped me to hit the ground running when the first team opportunity came along.

The highlight was a call-up to the England U19s Academy squad, coached by Mike, that faced the Aussie Schoolboys in December 2002. I played in the first Test at Knowsley Road, St Helens, and scored a vital try in an historic 28-22 victory – we were the first side ever to beat them. I remember brushing off quite a few tackles on my way to the line and that the Aussies were moaning about the ref all night. A few days later, the lads beat them again, 22-12, at Headingley, Leeds, for a first ever series win to rub it in.

That Aussie schoolboys squad contained players like Tim Smith, a future teammate of mine, Heath L'Estrange, Ben Hannant, Dimitri Pelo, Ashton Sims and Ryan Hoffman, while our side had five Wigan young 'uns in it: Chris Melling, Luke Robinson, Craig Barton, Bob Beswick and me. Mike called it the proudest moment of his coaching career.

One-year contract:
Gareth runs into
London in 2004

The year before that England Academy win, in 2001, I'd been on the Great Britain Academy side's tour to Australia to complete the amateur representative honours I achieved touring with Great Britain U16s and U18s.

When Mike sadly fell ill, his assistant Denis Betts took over as Wigan coach, followed by Ian Millward and Brian Noble, but Shaun Wane was undoubtedly the best coach I've ever played under.

Waney knew what made me tick. We were cut from the same cloth and the way he spoke to you made you feel ten feet tall.

Waney is a hard man, a terrific motivator and he rules with an iron fist. My drug habit finally stopped when Wigan put me on a specialist rehabilitation course.

It was what I needed, it saved my life.

My time at Wigan however stopped when I realised I had to leave my home town and start a new life in Australia ahead of the 2013 Season.

My first team career with Wigan had begun so brightly. At the end of that debut season I'd gone so well that I was named Super League's Young Player of the Year and won a place on the bench for the 2003 Grand Final at Old Trafford when Bradford turned us over, 25-12. Coached by Mike Gregory, we had a good team but didn't perform and we let the fans down.

That was also the year when I was included in the England 'A' squad to face the Australians at Griffin Park, Brentford, in October.

All of that earned me a new one-year contract that I signed in June 2004, but there were serious injury troubles just around the corner.

The first was medial ligament damage suffered against Bradford in February 2005, following an innocuous tackle by

Rob Parker. My studs stuck in the turf and my knee popped; it was a bad one. It needed a full knee reconstruction that kept me on the sidelines until the end of the season.

I battled my way back from it and looked set to return in 2006, but then sustained a stress fracture to the shin while running over the hills in Haigh Hall and had to miss the start of that season too. In total, I was out for 15 months.

I hate not playing.

Once fit, though, there were a fair few good times.

If you were going to ask me what I loved best during my ten-year spell at Wigan it would be facing Saints.

Their fans hated my guts, but the hostility gave me and Terry Newton especially an adrenaline buzz.

I never received any bullets in the post or shit like that, but as soon as I ran out at Saints you could feel the hatred.

I was a c*** in the eyes of the Saints fans – and still am. I have to smile.

Andy Farrell, Mick Cassidy, Kris Radlinski, Matty Johns, Terry O'Connor and Terry Newton of course were top teammates and belting blokes.

As it happened, I had to wait until May 2006 before making my long-awaited return from injury. It came against Salford in the Challenge Cup, a game we lost 16-4 but in which I personally went okay. It was a relief to be back on the field, especially as the game after that was against Saints.

Less happily, we lost again, 28-14, though I played well again and at least got over for a try this time. By the season's end I was in Great Britain's touring Tri-Nations squad, playing in the second row during a memorable 23-12 win over Australia in Sydney that November. It was the game when Aussie forward Willie Mason belted Stuart Fielden, breaking his nose and sparking a full-on brawl. In the other games, though, we lost twice to New Zealand in Christchurch

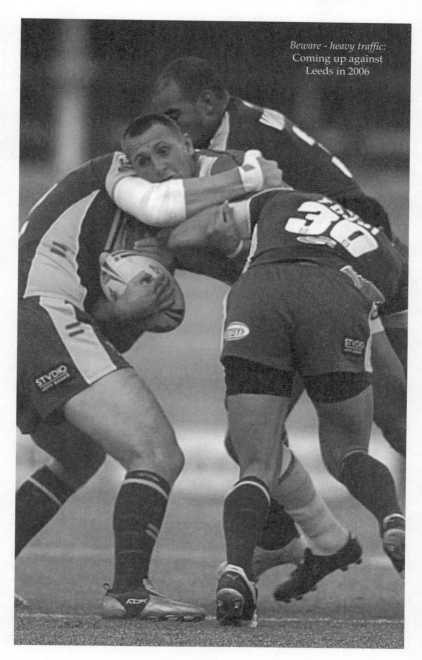

Beware - heavy traffic:
Coming up against
Leeds in 2006

and Wellington before being walloped by Australia in Brisbane and missing out on reaching the final.

It hadn't been a good season for Wigan either – we only managed to finish eighth in the table, not good enough by our standards.

The 2007 season was a bit better, we at least made the play-offs, but finished sixth and then fourth in 2008. My own form, though, was good and in October I was named in a 24-man England squad for the Rugby League World Cup in Australia. As a warm-up, we beat Wales 74-0 at the Keepmoat Stadium in Doncaster, where I scored one of our 14 tries, and then lined up in England's first Group A match against Papua New Guinea in Townsville, won – eventually – 32-22.

That game was a bit of a struggle, just as the whole tournament turned out to be. And after we were knocked out by the Kiwis in the semi-final in Brisbane we flew home disappointed under a bit of a cloud.

But that was nothing compared to the storm that broke with that failed drugs test in 2009, the low point of my career.

And two years later, when the ban came to an end, I had bulked up to 18 stone and signed a new contract with the club until 2015.

So all eyes were on me when that first game back came around in June 2011. We were playing Huddersfield at the DW Stadium – I felt like the fucking Incredible Hulk but was blowing from my arse after ten minutes.

This was the skinny kid who had started out as a halfback all those years ago and was now a Man Mountain.

I just couldn't carry the excess weight and didn't feel comfortable or at home in the propping role that our coach from 2010, Michael Maguire, was asking of me.

Running out wide was my forte and the hard work and sweat had to start all over again. Around two months later, we then played Warrington at the Halliwell Jones and I ended up being banned again for allegedly gouging Ben Harrison. Yes, I clocked him with a good 'un but I never went near his eyes. I have never been one for cheap shots.

Anyway I got five matches, which effectively finished my season.

That hurt, but Waney – at the time Maguire's assistant coach – was again there for me. He accompanied me to the hearing, calling the incident 'totally out of character'. I told them I was looking for a lever to help me get to my feet. As soon as I felt Ben's eyes I pulled my hand away immediately. They believed me but said I was 'reckless' and gave me a ban and a £300 fine anyway. Waney always knew how to get the best out of me but, as I said earlier, by 2012 the clock was ticking at Wigan even though I was on a big contract.

Joel Tomkins had switched codes and gone to Saracens, I was playing consistently well – as good as before the ban according to the pundits – so the number 12 shirt was pretty much my own. I know Waney, who was fully in charge by then, wanted me to stay, but off-field issues were piling up and there was a feeling in the air that I ought to pack my bags.

The result was that I met officials from Parramatta Eels at Wrightington Country Club and signed a two-year deal with an option for a third. A stint in the NRL was beckoning.

People had always said that my aggressive game would be ideally suited to that competition.

I was promised a house on the outskirts of Sydney, a car and various other perks. A big transfer fee was negotiated with Wigan and I was ready for off, but what I didn't know was that my partner, Danielle was pregnant with our daughter, Heidi.

The baby was due at Christmas, just when I should have been on my way to the airport.

Hock: The Real Me

French lesson: Taking on Catalans in 2007 with Thomas Leuluai

No way could I go, so I rang the Parramatta coach, Ricky Stuart to tell him I had changed my mind – he was fucking fuming. Stuart then got on to Adrian Morley, his mate from his time together at the Sydney Roosters, begging Moz to convince me to still go.

I couldn't.

Wigan thought I'd fucked them about too.

The club took £70,000 of my wages and sent me on a season-long loan to a club outside Super League's top four.

Widnes Vikings signed me. I had, of course, played under their coach, Denis Betts, at Wigan. He knew me and we were fine.

Kevin Brown, my brother-in-law, was already at the Vikings and he proved a great help.

I played well there. We only finished tenth in the table but I enjoyed my rugby league.

I'd had a few spats with Waney towards the end of my time at Wigan but nothing malicious. We remain great mates and I love a coffee and a catch-up with him.

In the end, Widnes did not have the cash to take me on permanently, but one man did – Dr Marwan Koukash at Salford – and a new door was about to open. In September 2013, I joined the Red Devil-ution on a four-year deal.

My Wigan days were over. And gone was the chance to emulate my hero, Andy Farrell.

Gaz Hock had flown the nest for good.

Salford had come calling and the Doctor persuaded me to sign.

Truth is, I still don't know the real reason why I had to leave Wigan, it was just one of those things that happens. Such is life.

My talks with Parramatta may well have influenced Wigan to find a suitable replacement, who knows?

Red alert: Working
hard for Salford Red
Devils in 2014

Devils may care...

4

Who'd a thowt it, as they say in Norley Hall – Gaz Hock signing for Salford. It happened though.

It still hurts to have left Wigan, but Super League's Mr Money Bags, Dr Marwan Koukash, was the man who enticed me to what seemed to be a club on the rise.

Joining the Red Devils at a time when all the 'Welcome to Hell' hype was at its height appeared a marriage made in heaven, but it would end in a very bitter and messy divorce.

With Wigan wanting me out, I agreed to be part of Marwan's multi-million pound rugby revolution.

It was show time for the success starved set-up and I was handed a starring role with the biggest contract of my career – a bloody good 'un in fact.

Marwan impressed me and other high-profile signings like Francis Meli and Tony Puletua with his ambition.

Hock: The Real Me

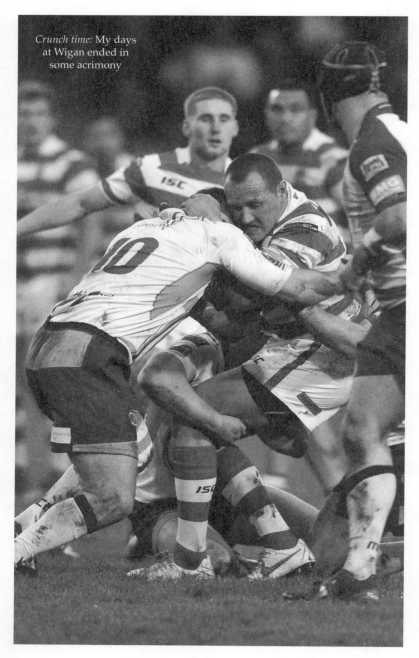

Crunch time: My days at Wigan ended in some acrimony

My old Wigan boss Brian Noble, the coach, wanted me and I first met club owner Marwan at his office in Liverpool.

I then made several visits to his palatial home in Rainford on the outskirts of St Helens.

It was like Southfork in *Dallas*. Massive security gates, top of the range cars on the drive and a massive pond. The whole place dripped wealth and luxury.

Marwan was a man wanting to build a team with the intention of overnight success. There were 12 new faces in all.

I was 29, I felt good. I was excited at the challenge and I got on with Noble. He is a decent coach who has always liked my style.

The club fixed me up with a luxury apartment on Salford Quays. A few weeks after signing me, on the eve of the 2013 Rugby League World Cup, Marwan was also magnificently supportive when England coach Steve McNamara sent me home from camp at Loughborough University for breaking a curfew. He slammed McNamara in the press and said it was disgraceful how I'd been treated.

My new teammates at Salford also included a couple of familiar faces in Tim Smith and Martin Gleeson, who I'd played with at Wigan. Apart from myself, the highest profile capture though was New Zealand-born halfback Rangi Chase from Castleford, who I had also played with for England.

I was in good shape and clean because my drug habit had long gone. I knew I had plenty to offer Salford.

As the start of the 2014 season got nearer, Noble took the squad to South Africa for pre-season training, but three days into the trip I was knocked back with the news of Keiron McNamara's death – my mate from Beech Hill.

I wanted to come back straight away but was told tests were being carried out on Keiron's body and it was pointless me returning.

So I stayed and trained hard. This has always been my style. I am not one for the glitz and glamour we were seeing at Salford.

Keiron's death played on my mind – it still does.

We kicked off a season of massive expectations against Wakefield and won 18-14. I scored a try and played well.

The following weekend we hammered London 44-18 at the Hive and some pundits were already talking me up as a Man of Steel contender. But then I knackered my ankle against St Helens in round three and was out for six weeks.

It came up like a balloon and it was not what I needed.

While I was out, things didn't go great. On Sky Sports, Phil Clarke had predicted we'd actually win the competition but that 38-0 home loss against Saints was followed by five more defeats with the only wins coming against Castleford and Bradford, so it was obvious things were going to be tougher than many of those experts predicted.

I returned to action, though, and got going again with a try in another defeat at Catalan. The club also signed New Zealand international fullback Kevin Locke. But by the time our home game with Hull FC rolled around in July, it brought another fucking setback I could have done without.

During the game, which being in decent form by then we won, 35-22, it was alleged that I deliberately ran into referee Matt Thomason – I bloody didn't. Even the overnight newspaper reports described the clash as accidental.

I was chasing a kick in the first half, running fast on a tacky surface, and couldn't avoid a collision with him.

I had to laugh. I hit him so hard the pea flew out of his whistle.

This was not my first run in with officials.

While at Widnes, I got a four-game ban for pushing referee George Stokes – or was it calling an in-goal touch

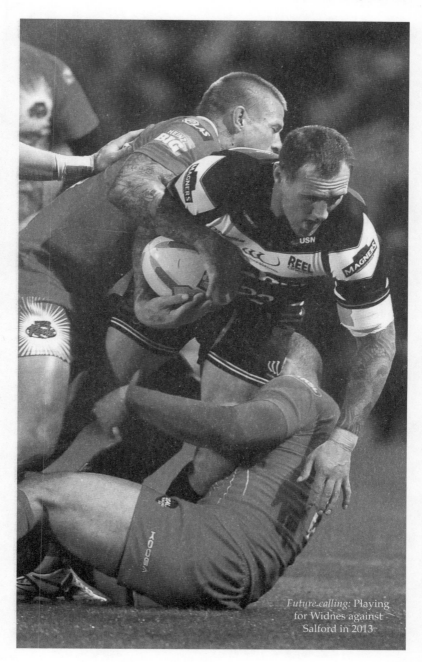

Future calling: Playing for Widnes against Salford in 2013

judge a prick? I can't remember. And back in July 2008, while I was at Wigan, I'd been given five games for 'manhandling' referee Ian Smith during a match against Huddersfield.

Seven games was my punishment for sending Mr Thomason skittling.

I couldn't bloody believe it – Marwan was fuming. Unless we made the play-offs my season was over. It was always an outside chance and, in the end, the lads only managed to finish tenth without me.

Anyway, by the time of that little bump at the AJ Bell Stadium, Salford had a new coach, Iestyn Harris, who replaced Brian Noble at the club.

At first he did give me some time off, but Marwan insisted I was soon back in full training.

After deciding not to appeal my ban, Salford also fined me for what had happened and I was livid.

As I say, I love playing and being sidelined for so long influenced me to put in a transfer request.

I skipped the last week of the season completely – fuck 'em I thought – I'd had a sickener of Salford.

They transfer-listed me.

Marwan made it quite clear he wanted to recoup the money he'd splashed out.

I actually spoke to Leeds and met the Rhinos coach Brian McDermott at Charnock Richard Services to discuss a move to Headingley, but nowt came of it.

There was even interest from French rugby union along with approaches from the two Hull clubs and Castleford.

The big asking price was a stumbling block. Marwan wouldn't entertain a loan deal.

As an astute businessman and thoroughbred racehorse owner whose horses have won such valuable races as the Critérium de Maisons-Laffitte, Cesarewitch Handicap and

Devil of a time: The sign says it all – I should have taken notice!

Ayr Gold Cup, Marwan is someone who is always texting his players, inviting them to his home and the races, and wanting to get inside their head.

He persuaded me to meet him for a coffee at the Thistle Hotel near Haydock Park Racecourse one morning and that's when I came off the list and reluctantly decided to give Salford another go.

In hindsight, I wish I hadn't.

But we talked of me playing 13 and being the middle unit. I fancied that and was with some good lads at Salford.

I had known Harrison Hansen from our time at Wigan and I also latched onto Kiwi pair Lama Tasi and Junior Sa'u, and Tommy Lee.

There was however one man I could not warm to – the coach, Iestyn Harris. He was cold and he kept his distance.

Hock: The Real Me

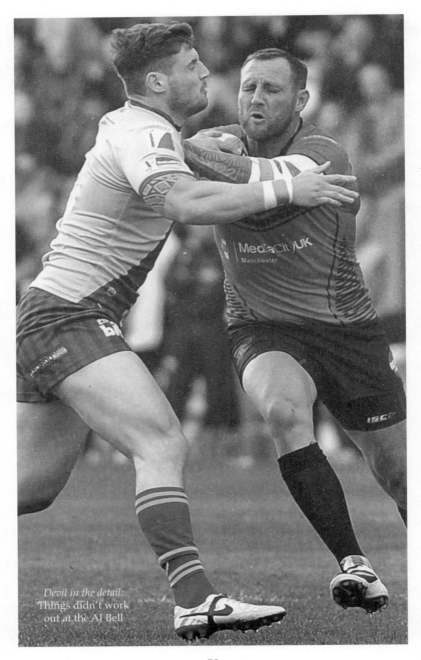

Devil in the detail:
Things didn't work
out at the AJ Bell

While at Wigan, I knew I could always talk to Shaun Wane, knowing he would listen. Harris was totally the opposite. I just couldn't take to him.

I would do anything for Waney, but Harris was doing nothing for me.

Harris had arrived at Salford from Wigan, where he had been assistant coach.

I struggled with the way he tried to get his point across.

It did nothing for me and a lot of the time I found it hard work listening to him.

I quickly got fed up.

On my return at Salford, we started the 2015 season away to Warrington, where we lost 22-8.

We then entertained Saints in a Thursday night match in front of the TV cameras and – just as had happened the year before – got stuffed, only this time by 52 points to 6.

But that wasn't the half of it. During the game, I found myself in trouble again and landed a crippling six-match ban.

Ben Thaler was the referee – I quite like Phil Bentham!

I was penalised twice for going in with the knees, first on Tommy Makinson and then sin-binned for a later clash with Mose Masoe.

The disciplinary panel threw the book at me, calling my actions 'reckless', but I still think a six-match ban was incredibly harsh. That would be my last game for Salford and February wasn't even out.

While I was at the club, no one ever openly labelled me a liability or told me that I was letting the team down with my indiscipline.

This may have been said behind my back, but what I do know is once again I had to get out of there.

Salford was not what it was cracked up to be and Harris was doing my head in.

I didn't like the way the club was run. I certainly didn't like the way we were paid and the coaching staff were not for me – they were doing nothing for me at all.

The conditioners, Richard Hunwicks and Josh Taylor, were good blokes and they did help – but Harris was doing fuck all for me. I did not care for either him or his methods.

I told Marwan I wanted out. He knew I'd had enough.

I told him I was going to retire as that seemed the only way I could escape from what was now a living hell.

I guess I am a complex character, but I can play.

Marwan offered me a job with his security firm, but the money was shit and I knew I still had a lot of rugby in me.

Retirement was never seriously on though.

I was nowhere near ready for packing in, but I kept telling myself I must wash my hands of Salford once and for all.

It had become a circus and I wasn't happy.

Harris didn't have the decency to wish me well when the time came to leave.

What also upset me were the cheap shots on social media from so-called Salford fans.

The keyboard warriors were out in force and I was sickened when some stooped so low they they started tarnishing the name of my mate, Terry Newton.

There was no need for it, but it shows you what people can be like and I snapped.

There again, none of this was said to my face.

I wouldn't like to say if Marwan was genuinely concerned about my well-being. He had been excited and supportive at first, but so much had changed.

What I will say is if Marwan really is worth a billion as is supposed, then the figure of around £40,000 I believe I was owed should have been buttons for a man of his wealth.

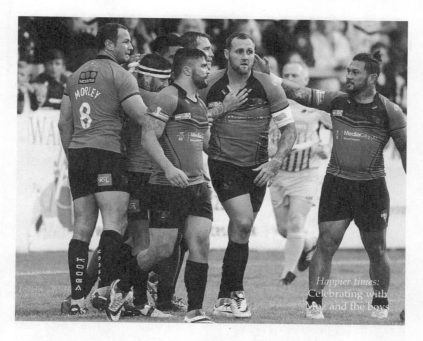

Happier times: Celebrating with Muz and the boys

Yet here I am still fighting for what was promised me and believe others have been in the same boat.

It was time to go – thank God.

Tony Smith, the Warrington coach, rang me about signing for the Wolves, but the wheels were already in motion for me to salvage my career with a move to Leigh.

Ay up, proud Wiganer!

Gaz was about to become a Leyther.

I was instantly impressed with the Centurions' owner Derek Beaumont, a real rugby man with passion.

Paul Rowley, the Leigh coach is also terrific – both welcomed me and made me feel at home.

I was so glad to get out of Salford, where I had fast been becoming depressed. Marwan was constantly contacting me offering an opinion and a view, but I'd had a bellyful and told him as much.

Not having a ball:
When Leigh called
I was happy to go

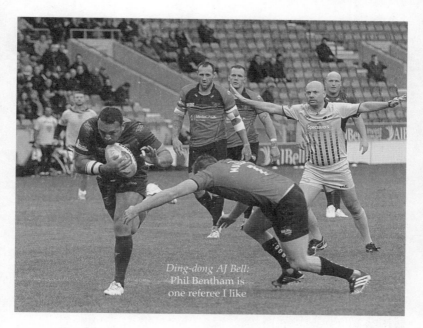

Ding-dong AJ Bell:
Phil Bentham is
one referee I like

But time moves on and there I was, free at last and ready to play for Leigh in the Championship.

It's a step down from Super League and I signed for Salford determined to be a success, but it never happened.

I can't pretend that isn't frustrating. And so is spending time trying to contact people at the club, chasing up various matters that have still not been resolved.

The day I left was a day I'll never forget.

Being out of the place gave me peace of mind and the chance to salvage my career.

I went to Leigh and was instantly surrounded by people who it is a pleasure to be with and alongside.

Under the guidance of Paul Rowley – I know I am in the hands of a good operator who, most importantly, listens and puts his arm around me.

This is what it takes to get the best out of Gaz Hock.

Moments of madness...

5

Yes, there have been plenty of the above! The red mist seems to come down and force my fists into action.

If I'm honest, my temper and my hot-headedness has always let me down.

Like most people I have done a lot of things I regret.

My anger issues surfaced at an early age and the stigma of violence has always been very central to my rugby career.

Referees have possibly had it in for me – give a dog a bad name, you might say.

The longer I have been in the game the worse it has got.

I'm a marked man and I'm drawn to trouble like a moth is drawn to a flame.

It has got to the stage where I'm now being sin-binned for being punched!

Banned from driving for three and a half years aged 16,

given 200 hours community service and an additional £800 fine... you could see the writing was on the wall from my youth.

Throw in the drugs and its one fucking big explosive cocktail.

I have never ever backed down from a confrontation.

No one has ever hurt or downed me and I've always been a handy lad used to aggression.

Mark Roberts was a lad I quickly latched onto in Worsley Hall.

He's a good sort who always looks out for you. He's not one of those shithouses who lives out of your pocket and then pisses off.

We played in the same academy team and were always good mates. He played at Pat's with Sean O'Loughlin and he remains a true and great friend.

As young lads at Wigan, we trained under Dean Bell and everyone used to say: 'Oh shit, watch your wallets lads. Here come the Kray twins,' when we rolled up together for training.

I absolutely hate losing and I guess this sparks my inner demons and pent-up frustration.

Teams and opponents are bastards for trying to wind me up. Sometimes it works and I just can't stop myself from lashing out.

I like a fight.

Paul Sculthorpe gave me a few cracks around the chops when I was a kid starting out at Wigan.

I've also had a few brushes with Ryan Bailey, another so-called bad boy, but we get on.

Keith Mason, who played for Huddersfield and Saints, used to strut around thinking he was Mike Tyson, but he was the proverbial Yorkshire Pudding.

Mason, a hard man? You're having a laugh. He put the handbrake on when he used to run the ball in.

I genuinely detest and despise Mason. Hitting him felt good. If he was in the room now I'd probably belt him.

I also remember a scrap I had in Manchester with Louie McCarthy-Scarsbrook – he's a gobby cockney now playing for Saints.

The mention of Manchester brings me round to my number one moment of madness – being sent home from the 2013 England World Cup Squad by Steve McNamara – another coach who I have absolutely no time or respect for.

We had played a warm-up game against Italy at Salford and lost, 15-14, thanks to a last-minute drop-goal from Josh Mantellato, who now plays on the wing at Hull Kingston Rovers.

That was embarrassing, obviously, and McNamara said no drinking on our return to the team's hotel at Worsley.

Some of the England lads, including James Graham, Sam Burgess, Micky McIllorum and Zak Hardaker, met up in the bar and decided to have a few drinks on the sly.

For fuck's sake, it was Saturday night and I had been going out on a Saturday night since I was 6!

A few other players joined us. Most of them had a drink and then went to bed.

The group I was with, though, chose to go to a Casino in Manchester and I drove.

We were back in for 3.00am and I was rooming with Rangi Chase, who I was looking forward to playing with at Salford.

He's not much of an alarm clock though. Rangi woke me up on Sunday morning and said: 'Gaz, get up now. The squad are going swimming.'

I fell back to sleep.

Hock: The Real Me

Internationals stalled: Getting up close with France at Hull in 2012

I wasn't pissed or hung-over, I just wanted a few more minutes in bed. After all, it *was* Sunday morning.

I eventually got up and heard McNamara say in a team meeting that a player was being sent home for breaking the curfew.

It was me who carried the can, yet McNamara didn't have the guts to tell me to my face that my World Cup was over before it had even started. I was going home.

I missed a ten minute swim – a ten minute swim for Christ's sake!

I ask you – no wonder I was fuming. I felt so let down.

I vowed there and then I would never ever pull on an England shirt again while this bloody man McNamara was in charge.

What he did with me was absolutely spineless.

I received a text from him saying 'go home'.

Fuck you, McNamara. That was my reaction.

I had been shit on, but why had he picked on me when others were equally as guilty?

I'd not been the only one who'd had a drink, but McNamara came down heavy on me and pointed his finger.

I think I know why. My name is Gareth Hock. I have a reputation. It's something I've learned to live with. It's got me into trouble but I don't hide from anyone.

The moments of madness have as I say been plentiful; there'll probably be more before I hang my boots up.

Watch this space!

Lifelong friend: The death of Terry Newton left me in misery

My best mate...

6

I burst into floods of tears when my mum rang me with the awful news that my great mate and lifelong friend Terry Newton had died.

I had been with him the day before he decided to take his own life, aged 31, on 26 September 2010.

I had even texted him only hours before he decided to end it.

Why the fucking hell did he do what he did?

He was one of the best.

Terry is the hardest and toughest man I have ever known. He was a fearless competitor and a true warrior who feared no man. He would part with his last anything for you.

Our paths first crossed as youngsters.

Terry went out with Stacey Parkinson, a cracking girl who was in my class at Tommy More.

They later married and Terry was playing at Leeds before he came home and signed for Wigan.

It meant everything to him to pull on a Wigan shirt.

We had many a cracking night out together. He was brilliant company. He lived life to the full and he played hard.

The last time I saw Terry, he was the Terry I'd always known.

No-one ever fucked with him. He would get in a few scuffles and some sticky situations at Wigan, but you never messed with Tez.

Those who did copped it.

He was playing hooker when I made my Wigan debut against Doncaster.

He would always say: 'All reet – I'm here and I've got you.'

He meant it.

I learned so much from training and playing alongside him. He was so brave and so incredibly battle hardened.

The Aussie's hated playing against him and he hated them.

He was one of those in your face players at all times but like I say he would do anything for you.

Terry was a tough street fighter. He had loads of bloody battles with many hard men from the Wigan area but he never ever lost.

He nearly went inside on a couple of occasions and, like me, he made the mistake of dabbling with drugs during what was a great career.

He regretted this – I know he did.

I will never ever hear a bad word said about him. Terry was like a big brother.

He was fast, constructive, destructive, formidable and forceful.

Pebbles on a beach: Here I am as a baby with my mum Kim, *below;* playing at the seaside in Rhyl; with my Auntie Tina, *bottom left;* and in a bit of a mess on holiday in sunny Spain

Father figure: Damian Hock is the man I think of as my dad – here he is going for the title of Mr Wigan, *left*, and in the Army, *below*

Family support: Damian's mum Peggy, *above*, my grandma and grandad, *right*, and mum and Damian – pictured with my son, Wade

Growing up: My High School years –
here I am showing off my physique,
above, where are all the tattoos!?!
And, *right*, a bit wet on summer camp

Schoolboy star: I was
only ever going to
play rugby league –
as I'm telling the
press here, aged 11

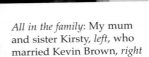

All in the family: My mum and sister Kirsty, *left*, who married Kevin Brown, *right*

Above: Kirsty meets TV soap opera stars Jack Ryder and Kym Marsh in 2001

Next generation: My son Wade, *above*, doesn't play rugby, but Danielle's son Lucas does. Here he is with Clock Face

Right: I was Super League's Young Player of the Year in 2003 – a proud moment

Here we go: Lining up with the Wigan town team – I'm third from right, front row. My full Wigan debut after coming through the systems was a dream come true

Making strides: My international call-up to the 2002 England Academy squad turned out to be historic. Coached by the great Mike Gregory, we actually beat the Australian Schoolboys in a series for the first time

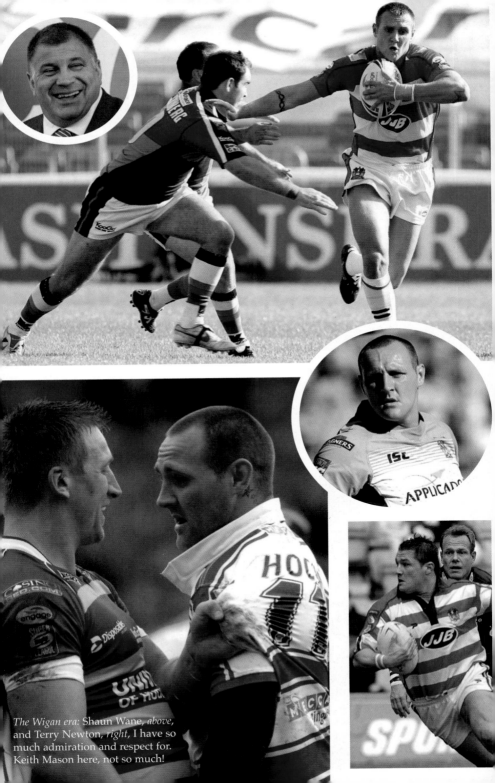

The Wigan era: Shaun Wane, above, and Terry Newton, *right,* I have so much admiration and respect for. Keith Mason here, not so much!

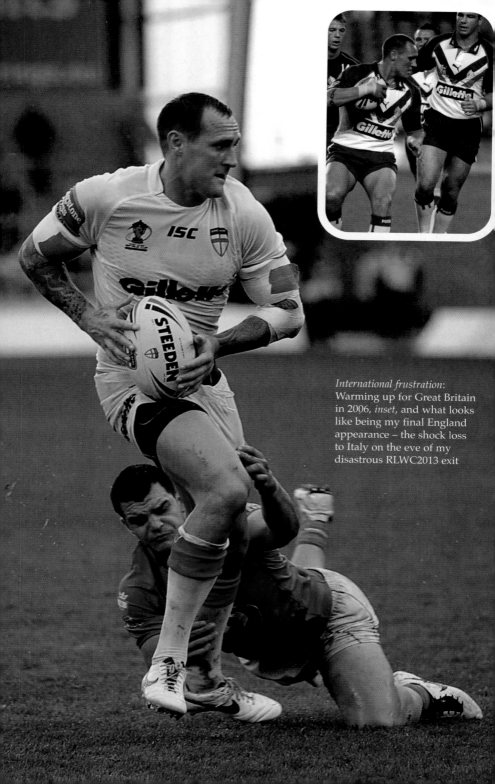

International frustration: Warming up for Great Britain in 2006, *inset*, and what looks like being my final England appearance – the shock loss to Italy on the eve of my disastrous RLWC2013 exit

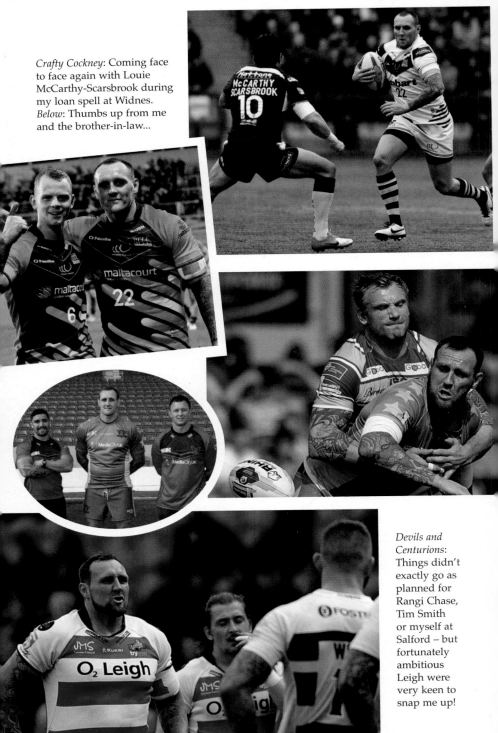

Crafty Cockney: Coming face to face again with Louie McCarthy-Scarsbrook during my loan spell at Widnes. *Below*: Thumbs up from me and the brother-in-law...

Devils and Centurions: Things didn't exactly go as planned for Rangi Chase, Tim Smith or myself at Salford – but fortunately ambitious Leigh were very keen to snap me up!

I will never forget one game against Saints at Knowsley Road. Boy did he give it Jon Wilkin good style.

He couldn't fucking stand Wilkin – from what I can gather, there are a few players in the game who don't care for him.

There's something about him – he's just so irritating.

Anyway, Terry gave it Wilkin full on with total venom and all hell broke loose. It was pandemonium.

Terry would also dish it out and give it Stuart Fielden in the scrum. He would wind him up by calling him names and he would goad him. Fielden always rose to the bait.

Newton's punching power was immense – it was awesome, he was like a machine.

He would defend anyone in his team.

I loved his company. He liked a drink and a good time, but he was absolutely super fit and so committed to the cause.

Terry was always the joker in the England camp.

He would take the piss out of anyone and would have me and Adrian Morley in stitches with his humour.

We laughed our heads off at the things he said and what he got up to.

On the field, he was totally focussed and fired up and so proud to play for his country.

I also remember the night in 2005 when he cleaned Sean Long out at the DW, in another feisty clash.

Although they were old mates and had grown up together on the Worsley Mesnes estate, they were not getting on at the time and Terry flew out of the line like a bullet and he nailed Longy.

Bang! The Saints man finished up with a broken cheekbone and eye socket, and was in need of reconstructive surgery.

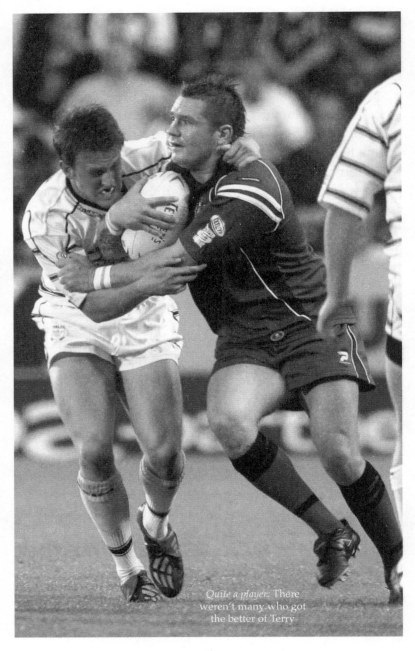

Quite a player: There weren't many who got the better of Terry

Terry had made his presence felt and minutes later he left Lee Gilmour badly concussed with another ferocious pile driver.

Not surprisingly, when both those incidents were combined he landed a record ten-match ban.

It was brutal, it came with the territory and it was trademark Terry, but you always wanted him in the trenches with you.

Sadly, in a tough sport like rugby league, time catches up with everyone and Terry's downfall began in 2009, when he started taking human growth hormone to speed up his recovery from injuries, injecting himself in his garage.

Someone had told him the drug was undetectable but it turned out not to be when, in November that year, testers turned up at a training session in Wakefield, where he was playing then, and took a blood sample.

In February 2010, he was told he had tested positive for HGH. He was the first athlete in the world to be caught doing so, which made news headlines everywhere. It landed him the mandatory two-year suspension, while his Wakefield contract was cancelled.

Terry knew his Super League career was over and wrote a book about his life, *Coming Clean*, saying that he'd like to help the UK Anti-Doping Agency in its campaign.

He never named names though, that wasn't his style, even though, if he had, it might have shortened his ban and allowed him to play again at a lower level.

I was at a bowling alley in Wigan with my missus and the kids when my Mum rang me to tell me she had heard Terry had committed suicide.

I was in a state of shock and immediately headed home trying to convince myself that what mum had been told was not true.

No fucking way was a man like Terry Newton dead.

Sadly he was and the rugby league world was stunned.

I still maintain suicide did not look on the cards, but Terry did what he did. We move on.

I went to see Stacey, who was naturally heartbroken. They had two little girls, Charley and Millie – Terry idolised them. I also spoke with his father-in-law, Keith Holden, at the pub they ran on the outskirts of Wigan.

I still couldn't believe any of this.

Stacey and Keith asked if I would carry Terry's coffin. I was honoured to.

Thousands of folk turned out at Wigan Parish Church to pay their final respects to this great player and great friend who had always done so much for me.

Terry was a popular figure in the game – you knew what he brought to the table.

I went to his house to pick up a few of his belongings and I geared up for the funeral.

I was losing a man I had loved and idolised – a man who had done so much for me, not only on the field but off it as well.

Terry was one of the few who would always listen.

I felt his death so much that I now have his name tattooed on my chest, with the words 'Rest in Peace Terry'. It is accompanied by a large cross.

His death left a massive gulf in my life.

Not a single day goes by without me thinking of him and all the good times we shared.

We had had so many laughs.

I even have a massive poster of him on my wall at my home.

I look up at it – it's from when we were together at Wigan – the greatest club in the world.

We were so proud and more than just teammates.

He was a rich source of inspiration and a true friend.

To have played alongside him was brilliant. I model my own game on his strengths.

To carry him to his final resting place so early on in his life was something I never imagined doing.

But life can be cruel.

Terry was taken way too early, as had been his sister, Leanne, who died after a battle with heroin addiction.

I'm forever indebted to Terry for simply being Terry and always knowing my back was covered at all times and in all situations.

I miss him so much and he will always be acknowledged as the man who made me the player I am.

I would watch Terry and be in awe of him.

So strong, so tough and so genuine.

Heart of the matter:
There is more to me
than trouble-making!

The soft centre in me...

7

Not many people know the real Gareth Hock. Not that I'm overly bothered. There are possibly many who don't *want* to know the real me.

Well I'll tell you, I'm a lad who will help anyone and do anyone a good turn.

That's how I've been brought up. I'm a big-hearted guy with a soft centre inside this mean exterior.

I'm certainly not a dickhead! I have a great family and a terrific circle of friends.

As this book goes to print, I have just got engaged to Danielle, who comes from Rainford. We have two children, Billy, who is three, and Heidi, who is 16 months.

I love Danielle and the kids to bits, they are my world. She is the best thing that has ever happened to me and I'm so grateful for the way she stands by me. She's perfect.

Hock: The Real Me

I also have a 12-year-old son, Wade Hock, who lives in Beech Hill. He was born with his bowels on the outside of his stomach but came through following surgery and is perfectly healthy now. Wade doesn't play rugby, yet the game was my life from an early age.

So many people get the wrong impression and are quick to tarnish me.

Away from rugby league, I like nothing better than chilling with the family and enjoying a glass of wine. I like to keep myself to myself.

All I've ever needed is people in my life who would listen to me – people who I could trust. In return I would do anything for them.

All things considered, I don't think I've done too badly from life and from rugby.

Stopping the drug habit was so important – vital in fact. Danielle has been so good for me; she is incredibly strong and supportive.

We met at a barbeque at my mum's house. Danielle is a friend of my sister, Kirsty, and we got on straight away.

Danielle is brilliant with the kids – a wonderful mother and partner. She taught our children respect, good manners and good behaviour at an early age.

I am so appreciative of this. I was expelled in the third year at St Mark's Primary School for fighting and sent to St Cuthbert's.

Danielle also has a son, Lucas who is nine. He is a good little rugby player. He plays for the amateur side, Clock Face, and I enjoy going watching them play. I treat him like my own son. He is a cracking little bloke.

When I have the time, I like nothing better than jumping into the car with the family and heading for the tranquility of, say, the Lake District.

Can we talk? I haven't always got on well with the press

It's good to get away from the daily grind.

Family life is so important and so special.

My folks have always stuck by me and I now like to provide for my own family.

It is so good seeing the children smartly dressed in nice clothes. They're happy and seeing smiles on their little faces and being with them is something money can't buy. I'm always there for them.

My mum works as a carer. My other sister, Cody, is a hairdresser and Damien, who I've always classed as my dad, works at Heinz.

Kirsty is a full time mum. As I said before, she married Kevin Brown, the Widnes captain, who is a great player and an equally cracking bloke. We are close, like brothers, and I really enjoyed playing alongside him at Widnes.

Kevin and Kirsty met when he dropped me off at home after training at Wigan. Kevin started his career there too and he hit it off straight away with my sister.

I've always had a great sense of humour – you have to as a professional sportsman.

I've been stitched up many times and I've also wound lads up.

As a kid, I robbed quite a few cars and was part of a 40-strong street gang who would sit outside the shops at Norley Hall drinking and making life hell for the police.

One night, we got involved in a massive battle in nearby Winstanley – I was locked up in a cell for 48 hours as a result.

I also remember scoring a try at Saints and throwing the ball into the crowd. The ball hit someone and it was claimed that what I did was deliberate. No way was it, but I still ended up at the centre of a CID investigation, having to explain myself. Fortunately, nothing came of that one.

I lived for a night out in Wigan, but it's years since I went up town. The bars and the streets are full of knobheads. I guess I used to be one but, at 31, I would take a quiet night in with Danielle and the kids anytime ahead of being legless in the early hours of Sunday morning following a King Street bender.

When I do go out, I prefer going to older pubs in the sticks and love chatting with the local characters – men like Little Mouse in Aspull – they all have a fascinating story to tell.

They are what I term proper folk and a reet good sort.

The old-timers love putting the juke box on and it's so good listening to the old American singer, Marty Robbins. The 1957 hit 'A White Sport Coat (and a Pink Carnation)' is the one that gets them up dancing and I've joined them!

Northern Soul and the sound of Motown are equally popular – get in there! But a night out in Wigan on the beer is no longer my cup of tea.

I appreciate home comforts and being with Danielle.

I used to enjoy caravan holidays in Wales as a kid.

I spent a lot of time there and at home with my grandad Bob, who is from Worsley Hall. He loves watching me play. I'm just a country boy at heart and I enjoy coarse fishing, but I haven't been in ages.

I'd go tomorrow if I could and may well give Josh Charnley a ring.

DIY is not my forte, but I'll swing a hammer and have a go when I have to.

I really like quality clothes and classy watches; I have a passion for cars. I can't watch football, it's crap, but I do take a very keen interest in boxing.

Asking to leave Wigan, the club I loved, is something I regret to this day, but you never know what is around the

Plenty of passion: The great Mike Gregory is much missed

corner, do you? The thing I miss most is the dressing room banter. That was always special.

Me and my mucker, Micky McIllorum, used to have so much fun together. We trained at Orrell and would regularly nab the keys and drive Eamonn O'Carroll's car and park it up on the nearby Water Park.

His face wondering where it had gone was a picture.

This would happen three times a week and any players' keys left lying around soon had me and Micky Mac swinging into action.

Terry Newton was king of the wind-ups. He'd ring up pretending to be either Ian Millward or Maurice Lindsay. I'd always fall for it and end up doing this, that and the other. Brian Carney took the piss out of everyone and used to give Martin Aspinwall a really hard time.

Martin was a clever lad but he just wasn't streetwise and Carney would ruin him. Carney would give it but didn't like taking it, although he ruined so many.

Cars were always a target, kit bags were another. I once had a training ground fight with Stuart Fielden. It started with a bit of slap and tickle and ended up with full-on fists swinging.

'Let em fight,' said coach Shaun Wane – the other lads looked on and were laughing like hell. We were eventually separated.

I have had my own leg pulled many times. When we played Celtic Crusaders in Wales, Terry Newton said I'd need to bring my passport, so I did and the lads didn't half give it me.

When I rolled up and they saw it in my bag there was uproar.

I also remember Mike Gregory taking us to see the Mel Gibson film, *The Passion of The Christ* in 2004. I think it was

Hock: The Real Me

Mick Hannan, who used to work at Wigan as the community manager, telling me that I would enjoy the film because he'd seen it.

Mick was a good stick – he said he didn't want to spoil the film for me, but pointed out that the main character (a bloke with a beard) got killed in the end.

Pull the other one, Mick!

You didn't get me on this occasion!

I greatly enjoyed playing for Mike Gregory and would go around to his house for my tea.

Mike, who died in 2007 after a four-year battle with a form of motor neuron disease, took a genuine interest in me and was a truly wonderful man. I miss him so much, as many people do. Mike was among those who would always listen and encourage me.

My liking for body art and tattoos is there for all to see – have a look on the cover! My body is almost covered – call me Beckham – I've spent a fortune on them.

I have two full sleeves, depictive images on my back and chest, plus there's still room for more.

The Terry Newton tribute one is my favourite and I don't mind the pain when having them done.

Peter Eccles from Wigan has done most of them and I've also visited a guy in Manchester who has done tattoos for Sam Tomkins.

My first one was a Chinese symbol when I was fifteen. Christ knows why I went for this, but I had it done when I was playing against the Australian Schoolboys.

It was the first of many.

Like I say, I'm always there when someone needs help. It's fair to say I'm possibly too soft at times. Many may find this hard to believe but it's true and I'll never ever see a mate either struggling or in trouble.

Holidays are normally spent in the sun with the family. Trips have always been memorable and eventful.

One pre-season trip with Widnes certainly was. We were up in the Lakes and went camping.

It was close to midnight and I was in a tent with Paddy Flynn. We started wrestling and things got a bit daft and out of hand.

Someone then burst into the tent, grabbed me and starting choking me: 'Let go, you bastard,' I yelled.

They did and it was our coach, Denis Betts. We ended up chasing one another around the campfire. It was absolute bedlam, the other lads came out of their tents saw us and started chasing us. We ran for miles.

I still laugh about it now.

I guess from an early age people have always come after me.

It still happens to this day, but I can laugh about it and I can look after myself.

You have to live life to the full and appreciate every single day.

Smiling costs nothing and I like being with the people who like me.

Those who know me best will tell you that the real Gareth Hock is a bloody good stick.

What's the saying? Don't judge a book by its cover.

That certainly applies with this one.

On Australian soil:
Playing for GB
down under in 2006

My finest hour...

8

Tez Newton used to say that there was no better feeling than smashing the Aussies and he was spot on.

I always loved a bloody, head-on battle with them because you wanted to test yourself against the best and come out victorious.

Back in 2006, I was part of Brian Noble's Great Britain team who went to Sydney and beat the Aussies 23-12 in the Tri-Nations, the game I referred to earlier in this book, when Willie Mason and Stuart Fielden took the headlines.

What a win - the greatest of my career.

It was the first time they had suffered defeat with Ricky Stuart in charge as coach and we had been written off as no-hopers in the build up to the game.

We were supposedly only there to make their numbers up. This inspired us and we used it as a motivational tool.

My finest moment:
Running out to face –
and beat – Australia

It worked a treat. Come the time to play, we were fired up and in their faces from the off.

It was a truly great and deserved win for us. Nobby was made up and I was feeling on top of the world.

At that time, I was playing the best rugby of my life. Running hard, handling well and tackling anything that moved.

Big Willie was trying to put himself about in the early stages. He had a go at Sean Long and it set a trend. This was Mason all over.

We were determined not to be either bullied or intimidated and gave as good as we got. We had some handy lads in our ranks who never ever took a backward step and could handle what was thrown at them.

I was in a formidable pack that had Fielden at prop alongside Jamie Peacock and Terry at hooker. What a front three – they were never ever going to take any prisoners and they met fire with fire from the start.

It was brutal at times, full-on combat, but this was going to be our night in Sydney. We were in the mood for both a fight and to play rugby.

The bulldog spirit was too much for the Aussies and they didn't like it one bit.

Ashley Klein was the referee. He used to take charge in Super League before moving to Australia.

Nowadays, Phil Bentham is always okay with me when he takes charge and at least he is one of the few referees who talks to players.

This particular Ashes clash was always on a knife-edge and it was simmering from the off. Tez was steaming in and with Peacock and Fielden up front we looked to dominate. I was in the back row with Gareth Ellis, while Sean O'Loughlin was in his customary loose forward role.

It was a big game for all of us. We had to stand up and be counted. We all did and we all put our bodies on the line for our nation.

I have always regarded it as an honour to play for my country until my very recent England fall out with Steve McNamara. That was a sickener, but the victory in Sydney was special and very much sweet revenge as the Aussies were just starting to get a bit too big for their boots and we kicked ass.

Darren Lockyer was skippering their side. He was a player who always seemed to cause us problems and grab them a win. We had to keep close tabs on him and we did.

Lockyer had Jamie Lyon and Greg Inglis outside him and home advantage of course. We were seen as lambs to the slaughter but came out fighting. It was nip and tuck for long spells, but we sensed our time had come.

Paul Wellens was at full back – and what a player he has been. I wish him well on his retirement. Wello has served the Saints magnificently and been a great pro. He played well that night too, was typically reliable and steady and got among the tries. Peacock also crossed the line. Lee Gilmour and Gareth Raynor added our other tries.

My old mate from Wigan, Brian Carney, was on the wing, with Keith Senior and Kirk Yeaman in the centres. They were strong and if you got the ball to Carney, a try was invariably on. Carney was rapid.

He was a joker in the pack but he could score tries. James Roby and Adrian Morley were on the bench, along with Jon Wilkin.

Longy played well at scrum-half and was partnered by Leon Pryce, a big unit as a six, and they combined well in Super League at Saints.

I have known Longy since being a kid. He is a character

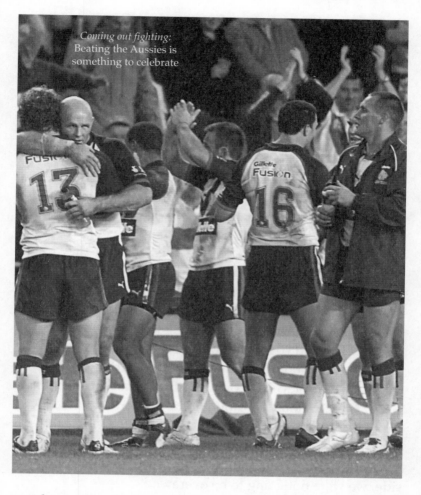

Coming out fighting:
Beating the Aussies is
something to celebrate

and he survived a few clouts from Willie Mason and made his mark. He bossed the show and had arguably his finest game for his country.

A week later, though, following our 34-4 loss in New Zealand, he was on his way home after having what the newspapers called 'a drunken binge' on our flight back to Australia. There must be something in the Wigan water!

In 2015, two of the game's all-time great players, Adrian

Morley and Jamie Peacock, hung up their boots. These are two top class players and blokes I have always respected. It really was a pleasure to play with them at international level.

They have been as good if not better than anything the Aussies have had over the years. To play alongside JP and Moz was always special - hard men who were so influential. They set the standard and we need more in their mould.

But the 2008 World Cup did not go according to plan. A few players just did not get on, I just tried to keep my head down. It is always a bit difficult when there are splits in the camp. As in life, not everyone gets on with each other and you are disappointed when a mate does not get in the side.

Players do tend to stick together whether they be the Leeds lads or your mates from Wigan.

I was ordered home early from the 2013 World Cup and Brett Ferres of Huddersfield took my place. This still hurts me because, as in 2008, I was feeling good. I would have liked to have achieved so much more at international level.

My stand-out club game was a Good Friday derby with Saints at Knowsley Road on 9 April 2004 that finished 21-all.

It was vicious, confrontational and brutal in fact. Karl Kirkpatrick was in charge and the fists were flying early on.

Mike Gregory was Wigan coach and he made us feel ten feet tall when we ran out. With Andy Farrell leading the side, we were not going to be overawed.

Faz really was Captain Fantastic. He was a truly world class player, so brave, but was also as hard as nails and a derby was his stage.

Faz played it hard but fair. He hated it when cheap shots were thrown and reacted as only Faz could when he thought an opponent was bang out of order. He would let anyone have it if he was narked.

He would regularly have a spat with Paul Sculthorpe.

They were the main players around at the time and Faz was Wigan through and through. I idolised him.

My future brother-in-law Kevin Brown was in the centre and scored a try for us.

Terry Newton was naturally in the thick of the action and he also powered in for a try. We looked on course to wipe the smile off the face of Saints coach Ian Millward.

Saints had led with a couple of tries from Lee Gilmour, who started out at Wigan. We refused to buckle. I had started on the bench but was seen seeing active service on what was a dreadful day weather-wise. It poured down during the entire game and this was a leveller. Some of the hits and the collisions were ferocious. More than just bragging rights were at stake in this one.

From an early age, any win for Wigan over St Helens was special. It applied at town team level and actually intensified as we became professionals.

Shaun Wane talks openly these days about his hatred for Saints. I know where he is coming from.

I always looked forward to the derbies. They had a special edge to them and were always uncompromising. Winning them was everything a matter of life or death.

The atmosphere is always special. The hairs on the back of your neck stand up the moment you come down the tunnel whether you are at home or away.

We thought we had won this particular game. Danny Orr was at scrum-half alongside Sean O'Loughlin. Faz kicked a drop-goal in the clinging mud and we were seconds from a famous victory when Longy did likewise to level. The little bastard had done us at the death. It was pure theatre with aggression and violence mixed in.

Terry O'Connor was propping for us alongside Tez and Quentin Pongia. Mike Gregory was so proud of the way we stood up to Millward's men and refused to buckle. The Wigan spirit was certainly on view that day.

Rugby league at the highest level can be a bit like professional boxing. There are times when you have to be defensive and soak up intense pressure. You then strike and cut loose.

This was the key for GB that famous night in Sydney. We celebrated a great win and it is something I will look back on and cherish.

As with international battles, blood was often spilled in derby games. Mick Cassidy, Danny Tickle and Faz formed our back three at Saints that day and they were strong, hardworking and resilient.

I can remember a host of closely contested derbies won either at the death or in controversial and dramatic circumstances. Something always seemed to happen.

This particular fixture was one of the hardest games I have ever played in. It turned into all-out war at times. Both sides gave their all and more. There was no let-up in the intensity and it felt like a win for us.

Mike Gregory greeted us in the dressing room and saluted our determination.

I enjoyed being part of the Wigan set-up under Mike. He was a local lad and he was honoured to be the coach of his hometown team. He was good and helpful when I played for him as an international junior. You could see then that he had what it takes to be the great coach he was.

It was tough to take when Mike became ill and could no longer continue coaching. I know what it meant to him because, like me, he has been in rugby from a very early age. He had gone on to enjoy a great playing career at Warrington and with Great Britain. He was another brave leader who played and graced the highest level.

Trust me, it is a wonderful honour to wear the Wigan shirt but it is also a terrific honour to represent your country. It is very much the pinnacle and the ultimate accolade.

This is why being sent home from the England World Cup squad hurt so much soon after I had signed for Salford.

As you'll have guessed by now, I have never been a fan of Steve McNamara. I always loved playing for Great Britain and England but after what McNamara did with me, I decided there and then the international scene was not for me while he was still in charge and calling the shots.

What's more, I stand by that decision.

Rangi Chase made a similar call when he was left out for what turned out to be a blockbuster semi-final with New Zealand at Wembley – or so I am told.

Being denied involvement in the World Cup hurt because I had prepared well and was ready to go out there and deliver.

We had a good squad. Quality stars like Sam Tomkins were on top of their game and the pack was very strong.

After being sent home, I simply did not have the stomach to even watch games on the TV. I felt let down and short-changed by Steve McNamara.

Marwan Koukash, the Salford owner, blasted him in the media and, yet again, I just had to pick up the pieces and move on. Marwan thought I got the mucky end of the stick. He was right.

All in all, though, I have lots to be grateful for.

I played with some great players at Test level.

And I played with some wonderful players at Wigan.

Feeling right at home:
Leigh Centurions is a
club that suits me

Leigh and life after rugby...

9

Me becoming a coach? Bollocks to that. I don't want any more shit from this game and I'm done with rugby league for good when the final hooter sounds on what will be my last match.

That will definitely be it. Time up. No chance of me either becoming an academy or junior coach and working my way up. I'm going home to Danielle and the kids.

I'm 31 now and I've no plans to retire just yet, but when my final appearance does come around, there will be no comebacks.

When I finish I finish for good.

I still feel fit though and know I have a couple more years left in me.

Leigh Centurions will be my last club.

Playing in Super League for them would be a bloody

*Viking on the charge:
I enjoyed myself very
much at Widnes*

good way to go out. A good way to complete what's been a long, eventful and exciting journey.

Playing rugby league is all I've ever done from an early age. Your body can only take so much punishment and I want to relax away from the hustle and bustle of the sport once I'm out and my boots are hung up.

The media have given me a very hard time.

I've been ridiculed at times by a few reporters – believe me I know who they are and I won't miss that lot.

At the end of the day, I'm just a normal decent guy and I feel it will be good to make a clean break and get out of rugby league and make a fresh start.

I will have had my day and my time.

I'm at my best when I'm happy and people are listening to me and hearing me out.

Yes, wrapping up really did cross my mind when things got bad at Salford at the start of the 2015 season, the end of my time there.

My head was all over the place and it was without doubt the lowest point of my career. For the first time in my life I was not enjoying playing a game I loved.

I feel there is no genuine passion at Salford from the top down to the supporters. I still keep in touch with a few fans on social media, but my appetite for the game was going the longer I stayed within that particular environment.

It wasn't for me. Signing for Leigh did me a power of good and thankfully got my career back on track.

They're a fantastic club with huge potential and what support *they* receive!

If only we could beaten Warrington in the Challenge Cup – we had a real good go.

Running out at the Halliwell Jones Stadium and seeing a sea of red and white behind he posts was so inspiring.

Leigh deserve to be back in Super League and I will do all I can to help them reach that goal, though it hasn't happened at the first attempt.

They bring so much to the table on and off the field.

I have felt wanted at Leigh from the day I walked into the Sports Village for the first time.

Great people who know their rugby are running the club and are genuinely ambitious. They have a top coach in Paul Rowley who, as I said earlier, I rate highly.

Playing for Leigh has renewed my hunger for the game and extended my career.

I was serving a six-match ban when I arrived at the club and so felt uncomfortable when I was paraded in a press conference.

All eyes were on me, but I realised there and then that Derek Beaumont and Paul had total faith in me.

I have since shed one-and-a-half stone and worked my arse off. I know I can still perform.

Signing for such a supportive and friendly club with Leigh's ambition and fan base was just what I needed after being out on a limb at Salford.

It has been a great move.

I now know I can pick up a phone anytime and speak openly to Paul Rowley. I appreciate this. It's good and it's something I must have.

Rowley is the best coach outside Super League. I like his style and he is heading for the top.

He knows all his players and you can talk to him.

I also like Derek a lot. He is Leigh through and through. He knows his rugby and takes care of his players.

Derek has looked after me and is incredibly protective. You can have a laugh with Paul Rowley but he has the ability to switch on and be deadly serious when that time arises.

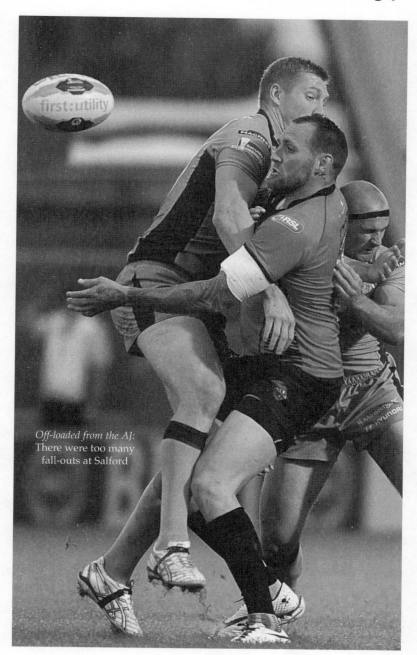

Off-loaded from the AJ:
There were too many
fall-outs at Salford

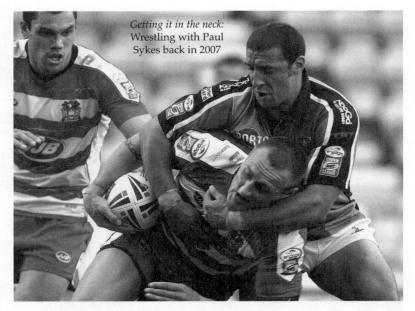

Getting it in the neck: Wrestling with Paul Sykes back in 2007

He is a shrewd tactician and a fine motivator.

When he speaks you listen and training is good.

I feel very much part of Leigh and their bright future.

What I will miss when I do hang up my boots is being with the lads on a daily basis.

Leigh is a family club, the ambition is there for all to see and the fan base is brilliant – many clubs would love to have this kind of support.

Rowley inspires and all the lads go out and have a real dig. Take Tommy Goulden. He is in his 30s and has been around the block, but credit to him for still mixing it and playing his socks off. He sums up true spirit.

Gregg McNally is a very underrated player who has impressed me and it is an honour to be playing alongside Fuifui Moimoi. We almost teamed up at Parramatta. We train together in our own time at Chorley. Fui is an absolutely brilliant bloke with a big heart. He will help anyone at all times and really is a larger than life character. Like me, he loves it at Leigh. The camaraderie is brilliant.

Leigh also play a damned good brand of rugby – which shouldn't be overlooked – and I like that.

All in all, I went pretty well in 2015 and I want to play for Rowley. I would still like to win a major honour though.

I regret never having played at Wembley, but I did play in a Challenge Cup final at Cardiff and I also appeared in a Grand Final at Old Trafford. I also played for Great Britain at every level. I gained England honours and represented Lancashire. I will be able to look back on many good times.

I'm still playing the greatest game in the world too.

I do however feel and realise the need to distance myself from rugby when I eventually retire.

The family will come first; Danielle will see much more of me. I have already set up a business – Zoo Performance at Preston – specialising in the sale of top quality sports and performance cars. Gareth Hock the businessman, eh?

I greatly enjoy this venture and have already invested heavily in it. I am giving it my all as I do with every challenge I undertake.

The business is going well, the potential is vast and it should be booming by the time I do hang up my boots and ride off into the sunset. This is the road I will be going down. Paul, Mike and Adam are my staff and I know I have a great, hard-working off-the-field team.

I feel I'm ready for this new challenge.

I guess I've come a long way since I was helping Ged Byrne on his window cleaning round in Aspull.

I don't mind hard graft and I've done everything I wanted to do in the game. Playing for Wigan fulfilled a dream, although a few Wembley appearances would also have been nice. Believe me, Leigh really wanted to be the first club outside Super League to go all the way to Wembley in 2015. Losing big games hurts – I know the Grand Final defeat for Wigan against Bradford back in 2003 certainly did.

I came off the bench but the game had gone from us early doors. The harder we tried, the worse it got. Tez Newton was in tears at the end. Like I have said, we let the Wigan fans down that night, but Bradford were machine-like at their peak. They always tried to steamroller opponents.

It's only when you pull on that shirt and run out in front of those supporters that it hits you.

A select band of people know what it means to be a Wigan player. I dreamed about this at an early age. I almost messed it up with what I did off the field, but I was thankfully given a second chance and am grateful for it.

Rugby league has been my life and it has kept me on the straight and narrow.

Aussie Darren Lockyer was the best player I ever played against. He was a bloody handful, brilliant, gifted, classy and elusive. You had to watch him like a hawk.

Sean O'Loughlin is the best player I have played with, along with Trent Barrett. Lockers is the ultimate leader. We came up together and trained hard together. He's a truly world class player.

People say he would've been a huge success had he gone to Australia – he definitely would. Players like Lockers stand out for their skill and strength.

Barrett was a winner and a wonderful footballer, but Lockers is the main man. He sets the standard – he's the man you look up to and will do anything for. You want him on the field with you. The bravery of the late Steve Prescott MBE also greatly impressed me.

As for the best coach I have played under, well that's pretty obvious: Shaun Wane.

Too familiar sight:
Sent off for Widnes
against Bradford

As a player I've always needed a coach with the ability to get inside my head and understand me. This enabled me to give something back to that person in return. It's a two-way thing, you can call it player performance, but Waney has always known better than anyone what s needed to make the real Gareth Hock stand out and star.

We have a long-standing mutual respect.

We are similar in many ways; two proud Wigan lads who come from the same background.

We also know that you have to be strong to survive.

You can call us born winners, but it's a fact we had our hearts set on playing for Wigan at a very early age. Nothing was going to stop us from reaching our goal. We were aware of the passion and the honour of being a Wigan player.

Our dreams turned to reality and we remain great mates. Thanks Waney for everything and for what we have shared and for what we have been through.

Long may it continue.

Weighty insults:
Away supporters
are after my blood

Facing my old mates...

10

'You fat bastard!' yelled the Salford fans. They were baying for my blood behind the sticks when I stepped out for Leigh Centurions against the Red Devils in the fifth round of the 2015 Challenge Cup, a match that was televised live on BBC1.

Verbal abuse aimed at me from the terraces was inevitable from that lot.

I did leave Salford under quite a large cloud but life goes on.

All eyes were on me when I turned out against my former club and I would piss on the chips of those giving me stick from behind the barriers.

We won 22-18 and victory was sweet – really sweet.

It was our day and yet we did not play to full potential.

We won though and that is what mattered most.

Winning really is everything in professional sport.

Losing riles me.

I only found out on the day of the game I was playing. This was one game I did not want to miss.

I did not have anything to prove but I had a few scores to settle.

Coach Paul Rowley said: 'You're in.'

Belting! Let's do 'em, I thought, and we did.

I had left Salford and signed for Leigh, but had been forced to serve another lengthy ban before I really got going with the Centurions.

This was not easy.

It was a challenge in itself, but I got there.

When you are sidelined for a long period of time, it is frustrating. I hate watching games. I have to be out there with my mates in the heat of battle.

Prior to the Cup match, Salford dug their heels in and said that an agreement had been reached which prevented me from playing against them for a year.

It was all a bit messy and I got caught up in the middle of the counter claims.

The mind games started as soon as the draw was made.

This game was always going to have a special edge to it and the stakes were high.

Derek Beaumont, the Leigh chairman, was adamant I would play and I did.

I am so glad I did play my part.

I was £30,000 out of pocket for playing, mind you.

Salford stopped money I felt I was still entitled to. It has led to me sending them a court letter.

I am still trying to settle the matter.

I still want the money I feel I am owed.

My last game for Salford had been against Saints and

it looked at one stage as if I might retire after landing another ban.

This did my head in but I knew I still had much to offer as a player and I have no doubt that joining Leigh is one of the best decisions I have ever made.

That Saturday afternoon in April, we took on a team who had been going quite well in Super League – a step above – and there was a real buzz around the town ahead of the big game. A lot of people saw it as a pointer to how the Championship clubs would go against top-flight opposition in the new so-called Super 8s at the end of the season.

That was for them to worry about.

Don't think we had lost our marbles, but the plan was for us, 'Little Leigh', to be the first club outside Super League to reach Wembley and play in a Challenge Cup final.

Rangi Chase was not playing for Salford.

The Leigh fans were up for it and in the build-up to the match, the Challenge Cup was on parade at a betting shop in the town.

Locals were putting their shirts on us winning and the buzz around town was incredible.

Getting up for a big game has never been a problem for me. The bigger the stage, the more I like it.

Playing though against lads who were mates was a bit strange, yet my mind-set was on reaching the next round.

Friendships went on hold. I had a job to do.

Leigh's ambition is there for all to see. Derek wants this club up there, challenging the best. He impresses me greatly with his drive and passion.

Everywhere, though, the self-belief was incredible and nothing could have stopped me from playing in this game.

We were at home and fancied our chances.

Cory Paterson, who like Rangi and Harrison Hansen,

Hock: The Real Me

Pointing the way:
Leigh Centurions
coach Paul Rowley

will be a teammate of mine again in 2016, though at Leigh, ripped in for Salford and ended up playing in the halves. He made his intentions clear in the first minute by clobbering Gregg McNally.

We knew what he had done.

He was a bit late if you ask me.

We also knew that Michael Dobson was going to pose us a threat. He is a clever Aussie who impressed me when I played with him at Wigan.

We had a decent combination there.

Good player Dobson, very creative.

But he was crocked early doors against Leigh, went off and played no further part.

This meant Salford were heavily reliant in the middle on young Theo Fages.

He played well and I rate Theo highly.

It's good to see him finally moving on from Salford too, to St Helens. He is going to be a future star and is a tough and talented little bloke, a determined player for his size and really plucky.

I got on well with him during my time at the AJ Bell Stadium. He was causing us problems.

Both sides were creating chances and I was nowhere near fully fit with being out for so long. But I did my bit.

I sensed strong team spirit at Leigh from the moment I arrived at the club and it is vital in the make-up of any set-up striving for success.

Spirit was certainly strong against Salford.

Bob Beswick had a good game and Tommy Goulden – who never gives less than 100 per cent – ran his blood to water as usual, a cracking player.

Liam Kay ran and finished well.

We poached a couple of killer, crucial tries.

The breaks went our way, we scored when it mattered and a famous four-point win was secured. We sang our heads off in the dressing room afterwards.

Our confidence could not have been much higher. Salford were poor and we knew we were not at our best.

Paul Rowley said as much after the game, but the win delighted him and we progressed.

Aspects of this game were unreal considering the circumstances, it had all been 'will Hock play or won't he,' but we were in the hat for the next round.

It was a bad defeat for Salford.

I had the last laugh on a few people that day.

Our reward for beating the Red Devils was a trip to Wakefield, who were struggling at the bottom of Super League and against who we again fancied our chances.

There is tremendous confidence within and running through the Leigh camp and my old mate Tim Smith was calling the shots for the Wildcats.

He ran the show early on and we trailed. I twisted my knee and struggled but a remarkable second half turn around produced another thrilling win, 36-30.

We were again on TV and the fans had turned out in force. They willed us on and we won.

This was some performance and a clear sign of Leigh's intentions and ambitions with many saying we had breathed fresh life into the Challenge Cup itself, a competition that had gone stale in recent seasons with hardly any upsets anymore.

Some of the tries we scored were breathtaking.

Bob Beswick again shone.

I like to play an attacking brand of rugby and this is very much the case under Paul Rowley.

There is a never say die attitude in the camp.

Since going down to the Championship, I have noticed

that a few teams have had a go at me. I try to stay cool but it's not easy when someone belts you in the face.

With two Super League clubs accounted for, we really did start to fancy our chances of going all the way to Wembley.

Why not? We were in the quarter-finals.

We wanted a home draw but ended up going to Warrington – I always enjoy playing against the Wolves.

They had a sniff around me when I left Salford but talks were at an advanced stage for me then to join Leigh. I played for England under Warrington coach Tony Smith too.

If the games against Salford and Wakefield were tests – we'd also beaten London Broncos 64-12 in round four – this was a step up again. Yet we were not fazed taking on one of Super League's heavyweight clubs in their own backyard.

We have good players in our ranks, plenty of fine footballers and strong, determined forwards. The young lads are also talented and hungry.

Pundits had little doubt we'd be in the game early on, but wondered whether we could still stand toe to toe with Warrington in the final quarter.

This would seemingly be our biggest challenge yet.

As things turned out, we did do well early on, so much so that we led 14-12 at half-time and were good value for our lead. We were 40 minutes from glory and Wembley was beckoning.

I have some good mates in the Warrington ranks.

Ben Westwood is a workmanlike forward who is as tough as they come. We have had some good battles over the years.

We knew Warrington would come back at us and they won the game, 34-24, with their strong start to the second half.

The third quarter was our undoing.

A couple of tries meant we were up against it but we again hit back.

You can never write Leigh off. I was pleased with how I played but was bitterly disappointed to see us get pipped.

We were defeated but not disgraced and won many admirers, being on the telly again, and it kept a spring in our steps in the chase for promotion.

The support we received that day at the Halliwell Jones Stadium was unbelievable

I think the Leigh fans are still singing their heads off.

They almost raised the roof.

It is surprising how it lifts a player when you run out into what can be an intimidating away arena and see your loyal fans have travelled in numbers.

The away end was crammed with red and white scarves and banners.

I may well have copped a bit of stick from the Warrington fans, as I did when we faced Salford, but on this occasion, I couldn't hear it.

I'm not liked on many away grounds.

I wonder why?

The atmosphere was special at the HJS for a cracking tie and the day could have been equally as momentous.

The lads still talk about the Warrington clash. We could have won, had the chance to, but they struck when it really mattered.

The Challenge Cup is a competition that has not been overly kind to me over the years and our Wembley dream was over – in 2015 anyway!

I had really fancied a Challenge Cup Final appearance but it was not to be. We gave it our best shot. The Leigh lads do that every time they take the field.

Players like Tommy Goulden can't do anything else but have a dig. We are a team of incredible competitors.

And Paul Rowley is still busy putting together a good squad. We prepare well and know what we are capable of.

Leigh is a very progressive club heading in the right direction.

We really thought we were off to Wembley in 2015.

We fell short of course but at least we spoiled Salford's party and that will do for me.

The abuse I took from their fans back in April is water off a duck's back.

You get used to it after all this time.

This comes with the territory as they say.

It never stops and it never goes away but I have never been one to go hiding, however teams wind me up.

My career has been quite a journey and so too was this latest Challenge Cup campaign.

When I hang up my boots, I won't have any regrets but would have liked more medals.

If only...

Testimonials

A s someone who likes to keep himself to himself, I'm not used to doing all this talking.

So I thought I'd give you a break for a bit, with a few pieces that my ghostwriter, Neil Barker, has gathered from people who have a fair bit to say about me!

Many of the following pieces contain the words of people who are very important to me or maybe guided me through my playing career in very important ways.

I hope you enjoy reading them and will see you on the other side...

The finest coach:
Wigan's Shaun
Wane is a loyal man

Part of Wane's world...

11

Wigan Warriors' head coach Shaun Wane is firmly of the opinion Gareth Hock would have had a huge impact playing for the top Australian club in the NRL.

Wane has worked closely with Hock in the past and first spotted his potential and proven talent when the rising star was coming to the fore as a junior player.

Wane says: 'I have always had an affinity towards Gaz – he is a good bloke and a top player.

'We are very similar in our upbringing. There was a need for me to take an interest in Gaz, a need to look after him and help him develop as a player.

'Everyone knew he had a wild side and a tendency to self-destruct, but here was a Wigan lad and a special player.

'All he ever wanted to do was play for Wigan. And when I first saw him as a junior I was instantly impressed.

He was strong, talented and he stood out in games. It is not in my nature to give up on lads like Gaz and I didn't.

'As a bloke, he is a fantastic fellow who would help anyone. The same can be said about another tough and talented lad like this who also came through our systems at Wigan – Micky Mcllorum.

'I am saddened somewhat that our great game of rugby league never saw the best of Gaz Hock because he had so much and more to offer.

'We deserved to see the best of him because he really is a devastating player and we have only seen this in spells.

'I honestly believe he would have killed it in the NRL had he gone out to Australia.

'His game, his style and his aggression means he is ideally suited for this style of rugby.

'He would have relished the challenge and the competition and would have come into his own as other players have done. A fully-focussed Gaz would have done very well.

'I have always got on with him. Gaz has the toughness as we now see in Micky Mac – these are lads who play hard all the time and always want to win.

'He is also like Sean O'Loughlin in being able to operate strongly and highly effectively as a top forward, but also having the skills of a really good halfback.

'Gaz has a good skill level. We have seen a number of our top players go over to the NRL and impact. Gaz would have been among them had he ever gone.

'He has always had everything you look for in the make-up of a top class, fearless forward.

'Gaz has always been a handful for the opposition. You could see this in him at a very early age. We have always got on.'

Wane himself came up through the town team ranks, showed great potential as a schoolboy player and became a top forward.

Former Great Britain, Leeds, Dewsbury, Bramley, Halifax, Bradford, Workington, York, Keighley, Prescot, Lancashire Lynx and Wigan coach Maurice Bamford fondly remembers the big man having an early spat with Hull hard case Len Casey.

Wane was only a teenager at the time and yet Casey still ended up on the floor in the Central Pak mud.

As with Hock, Wane was highly honoured when the day came for him to sign professional forms and see his dreams turn to reality.

Playing and now coaching Wigan means the world to Wane.

His honesty is always there for all to see and as Hock has said many times, the Warriors' hard-working boss best knew how to get the best out of him.

It is easy to see why Wane now speaks so highly of Micky Mcllorum, another all-action robust, top class hooker who Hock views as the best in the world.

Wane likes his players to be brave fearless and to know what it really means to step out in front of thousands in a famous cherry and white shirt.

Hock and Mcllorum certainly tick all the required boxes. Putting their body on the line comes naturally to such tough competitors.

Hock made his senior debut as a young buck and was chomping at the bit when given the nod. The two tries he scored against Doncaster left his club bosses purring with delight.

And not only club bosses. Wigan legend Bill Ashurst was among the first batch of top class British stars who were

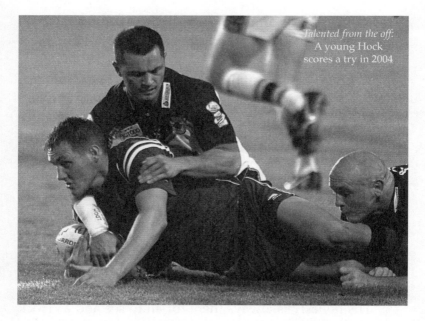

Talented from the off:
A young Hock
scores a try in 2004

enticed to face the best in Australia. Bill, a bustling back rower and hard man himself, returned from Penrith a hero.

He scored tries over there, traded punches and left with his head held high.

He had also played alongside the current Salford Red Devils coach, Tim Sheens, who was a talented ball-playing prop with the Panthers.

Ashurst, who like Hock had a wonderful running game, great hands and feared no one, went into the back row and instantly made his mark.

Nowadays, he remembers first watching Hock playing in Shaun Wane's junior team at Wigan and has no doubt he would have been a sensation down under.

'It does feels really good whenever you pull on the Wigan shirt. Wigan lads only want to play for Wigan. When you do land the chance, it's a very special feeling and you could see it meant everything to him.

'The NRL experience could have been the making of Gaz because the discipline is better over there.

'Players are also in the spotlight all the time. If you blow your nose, everyone in Sydney knows about it. Players are high profile like the Premier League footballers are in this country.

'You are focussed at all times at that level and you want to show the Aussies what you are capable of.

'Gaz was a great player as a kid and he did fulfil his potential. You knew early doors he was heading for the top.

'He could certainly play, he could mix it and the NRL would have been so good for him. He would have taken his game to new levels. We all know what a devastating player Hock is.

'Gaz would also have liked and enjoyed the lifestyle. I wish he had tried his luck over there because he had the game to smash it.

'He would have done just that.

'Gaz has never changed his style of play. You want him in your side and you know what you are going to get from him.

'The Aussies are always waiting for us Poms when we go to the NRL. They were for me, but I loved it and relished the competition against the best.

'I know Gareth would have held his own and he would have been up there with the very best.

'He is one of those players I have enjoyed following.

'Gaz is a good player – very strong.

'I really do think that not going to Australia was a missed opportunity on his part.'

Widnes family:
Brother-in-law
Kevin Brown

Keeping it in the family...

12

Gareth Hock knows what quickly gets under Kevin Brown's skin and makes his blood boil.

The talented Widnes Vikings play-maker hates it when he hears people, including players, either calling or smearing the name of his illustrious brother-in-law.

Brown says: 'It really does get my back up when I hear someone saying Gaz is a this, that and the other.

'I know Gaz is not an angel, but he is simply a tough player who plays hard .

'He plays the game on the borderline and sometimes he does go outside the rules but he is playing so hard to win.

'When they call him, many people just don't know what he is really like and this is what I try to get across to them.

'I hear them calling Gaz and have to say: "Hang on a

minute, let me tell you what he is really like and what a fantastic player he is."

'He is a top bloke and a brilliant player who is still doing what he has always done best.'

Brown is regarded as one of the most gifted players in Super League – a throwback to the days when nearly every team had a clever midfield dynamo who could make a ball sing and split the tightest of defences.

Hock says he and Brown are close – very close in fact – more like brothers. The respect and admiration they share is plain to see.

Like Hock, Brown was a schoolboy star courted by scouts because of his natural ability and vast potential. He played for Thatto Heath, Haydock and Pilkington Recs and was a target for a number of clubs.

Wigan managed to pip Saints for Brown's signature and he and Hock came together under the Warriors' banner.

Kevin later married Gareth's sister, Kirsty.

'I have nothing but respect and admiration for Gaz,' Brown continues. 'I could soon see he feared no one and would take a game to any opponent.

'He just ran as hard as he possibly could every time he had the ball. This was his direct style and this is where his aggression came into play.

'He is not only a power player, he also has fantastic skill levels. You cannot help but marvel at these. I have seen him do some incredible things with a ball in his hand. He is so gifted. I consider myself a ball player and there have been times when I have watched Gareth and wondered how on earth he did what he did. He has so much talent.

'Off the field, too, he is great company. He is incredibly tough and it's great to see him enjoying his rugby again with Leigh and playing well.

'Gaz is such a strong player. No one scares him and he can mix it with the best.'

Brown and Hock quickly impressed their Wigan coaches as they progressed on the ladder towards first team status.

Wigan have a reputation in the game for giving young players the finest grounding, not only in the fundamentals of the game but in readiness for a professional career.

Legendary Kiwi centre Dean Bell was among those who oversaw their development.

Hock always knew rugby league would be his ticket to step out on what has been a remarkable journey.

Kevin Brown adds: 'I was chatting the other day with Danny Tickle and I told him that Gaz really had such a great story to tell.

'His life really has been like a soap opera with so much happening, but he has always been strong.

'It is only when you stop and think that you realise just how much has gone on and what has happened over the years.

'It is fair to say that Gaz is very often misunderstood and misinterpreted. As his brother-in-law, I think I know him better than most.

'He is great company and a top man. He also has a wonderful sense of humour and is one of the nicest guys you could ever wish to meet.

'We all know what he is like on the field. You won't change him, but he is very much the family man who would help anyone.

'I like being with him. You have to be on the field with him to see at first-hand how strong and direct he is.

'You will never ever find Gaz taking a backward step. Like I say, he is absolutely fearless and a real competitor.

'He has played against the best and they have not been able to handle him such is his size and power.'

Former Wigan boss Maurice Lindsay has often said if a team was being selected to take on the Aussies, Hock's name would be one of the first to go down on the teamsheet.

Hock was long and rangy as a kid and he was at home at scrum-half. Heads would turn on the touchline as the town team marched to glory thanks to another supershow from the heroic Hock.

Raw-boned power has always been central to Hock's artillery and that continues to this day.

Brown and Hock were seen as the shining lights in a Wigan team going through transition and struggling somewhat following a decades of dominance.

Relegation looked on the cards at one stage with Ian Millward at the helm.

The Aussie known throughout the game as 'Basil' had coached Leigh and transformed Saints into the sport's major force, but Wigan was a different proposition. Youngsters were thrown in at the deep end by Millward. His team struggled.

Warriors' fans never really warmed to Millward – Hock himself was not overly keen – and so in April 2006 in came former Bradford boss Brian Noble to answer an SOS from worried club bosses.

Arriving soon after Millward's sacking, Noble took over at a point when the relegation battle seemed lost, however turned it all around and kept the Warriors in Super League on the back of a number of impressive performances.

Noble owed a large part of his success to his reliance on players with Hock's proven pedigree.

As an experienced coach and former hooker, he also knew what was needed to secure pack power. Noble liked Hock's formidable presence wide out – he was effectively an extra centre with strong defence – ideal material for the international arena.

Noble has since said that far more international honours should have come Hock's way than the 12 Test and World Cup matches he did manage. And those who played with Hock at his peak instantly back this up.

Former Great Britain scrum-half Sean Long, for example, is firmly of the opinion that Hock had much more to offer against the world's best.

'Gaz came often into his own playing for his country,' Long says.

'He was so tough to play against. Stopping him was near enough impossible at times. You won't see many finer players than Gaz. A Gaz Hock on his game was awesome.'

Brown and Hock's paths were further entwined when Hock opted against going to Parramatta and went to Widnes in 2013 on a season-long loan instead, just as his Wigan team-mate Lee Mossop *did* decide to undertake the new challenge and set off on a 12,000-mile journey.

By which time, Brown was nicely settled in at the one-time Naughton Park, then the Halton Community Stadium, having helped to revitalise Huddersfield Giants on his own earlier move from Wigan there in 2006, before arriving at Widnes six years later, in 2012.

Brown's silky skills have lit up many a close contest. The wiry stand-off stood tall for the Giants, who also had the nuggety scrum-half Luke Robinson on their books.

Robinson and Gareth Hock had both signed on the dotted line for Wigan when they were 11, with Luke turning up at Huddersfield, via Castleford and Salford, in 2008. The Giants brought out the best in both lads and certainly helped to lift Brown's game to the next level.

Of Wigan's five brightest academy hopefuls then – Sean

O'Loughlin and Martin Aspinwall (who, like Brown, was also turfed out to Huddersfield in 2006) being the others – only one, O'Loughlin, ended up staying the course.

When Hock landed at Widnes, it was seen as a quality signing and a statement of intent by the club, but also a bit of a gamble. Still, legendary stars such as the great Alex Murphy welcomed a lad who was prepared to play it as he saw it.

Murphy claimed that 'robots' were dominating the sport, yet such a label could never be bestowed on Hock and his talented brother-in-law Kevin Brown.

From an early age, Hock's style was simply to do everything in his power to cross the opposition tryline.

Unstoppable – unplayable at times – another Wigan legend, Denis Betts, and his coaching assistant Mick Cassidy were now to benefit from the Brown/Hock combination.

Betts and Cassidy had packed down together in the glory years for Wigan and were now busy trying to revitalise the former cup king Chemics. With Doug Laughton and a galaxy of international stars long gone, it was left to Hock and Brown to be the catalysts in a building programme for the ambitious Vikings.

Hock enjoyed the buzz of having Brown as a teammate, describing him as 'pure class'. The trademark breaks and off-loads soon had his ever-alert brother-in-law backing up and scooting clear to score.

Hock called Brown 'one of the best and cleverest players in the game today,' adding that 'he reads a game superbly, makes play happen and is a proven match-winner.' That he is, and it helped Hock to play well at Widnes.

It also helped that there were plenty of other good lads in the side, along with a coach who knew what he was getting with Hock and did a good job with him.

Stars of yesteryear are quick to heap glowing praise on

both Brown and Hock. The astute football brain of the quick-thinking Brown went hand-in-hand with the middle unit dominance Hock secured. Nowadays, Brown is still driving the Widnes machine in the same manner, with many considering him unlucky not to be in Steve McNamara's England set-up. Hock, meanwhile, is shining for Leigh.

Yet the former still relishes his time alongside the latter on Widnes's so-called iPitch.

'It was about eight years since we had played together at Wigan when Gaz arrived,' Brown says. 'He was out injured when I left to go to Huddersfield.

'I told Denis about Gaz's possible availability and the pair of us first lined up together again against Hull, who we absolutely destroyed. We hit it off straight away.

'I remember we caused so much damage down the left edge. He was steaming onto the passes I was putting out and it was like having a bodyguard.

'He is what I term an intimidating enforcer and he has a presence about him.

'Gaz could instil so much confidence by simply being on the field with you. He may have been having a quiet game, but knowing he was there was such a boost.

'I remember us watching a video of a match once and Denis wondered why Gaz was chasing around the field trying to get hold of Stuart Howarth.

'Gaz said he thought Howarth had elbowed me when I was down on the ground. This is what I mean about him being so protective and doing anything to help his mates.

'He always sticks up for you and sometimes he goes a bit too far, but every tackle and challenge matters to Gaz.

'He is the complete competitor who hates losing. It was so good to be alongside him again.'

The three chiefs...

13

Maurice Lindsay is convinced that Gareth Hock could have been up there with rugby league's all-time greats but for his strong tendency to self-destruct.

As in these pages, Hock himself admits that such a character trait has often let him down and landed him trouble on various fronts.

Lindsay, on the other hand, remains supportive of the local lad whose talent surfaced at an early age and marked him down as a certain star.

As a former Wigan chairman, Lindsay enjoyed watching Hock emerge. For as long as he was able, he also took great delight in making sure he formed the backbone of international sides taking on the Aussies.

Lindsay knew Hock had the skill and the steel to instantly strike fear into opposition hearts with his robust style.

Maurice says: 'I can still remember when he first came to the fore as a 14-year-old; he had everything back then.

'Hock was quite simply sensational. He ended up playing in the Wigan academy a year later and brought so much to the side. Hock stood out. He combined an ability to take the ball in as a prop would do, but added natural ball playing skills to this.

'It was incredible what he could do. I always tried to be like a father figure for him, offering advice and always encouraging him. He could pass the ball like a centre and had so much talent.'

Lindsay has often been quoted saying that Hock, who could play anywhere if he put his mind to it, had the potential to be one of the finest players in the world.

Had he gone to the NRL, Lindsay feels that grounding may well have moulded him into the complete player.

That was certainly the case for Sam Burgess at South Sydney and James Graham at Canterbury Bulldogs.

Lindsay also sees Hock's departure from Wigan as a big mistake. And had his own stay at the club been been longer – he stood down as chairman when the club was taken over by new owner and chairman Ian Lenagan in December 2007 – is convinced he would have been able to help Hock further.

Another man who helped Hock's development at Wigan was juniors coach Brian Foley.

As we have seen, he took Hock under his wing at an early age and was one of the first to see his all-round skill and talent. Foley worked hard to keep the young buck on the straight and narrow.

It was a challenge for Brian, but one which he relished and enjoyed. The pair still keep in touch. Foley has a great reputation in the game for developing talent and being protective of young players at all times.

Hock himself has described him as '...a top man, one of the best in fact. I guess he always knew how to handle me and there was total respect at all times.'

Though Lindsay admires Hock's abilities hugely, he also viewed it as a challenge to work with the player. And the same could be said for the coaches whose job it was to put him through his paces in training.

Lindsay made it clear to former boss Ian Millward that he would help Hock at all times on and off the field.

Hock was certainly Brian Noble's type too – tough uncompromising and direct. Which is exactly why the one-time Great Britain boss later brought him to Salford.

Harrison Hansen, a teammate at Leigh in 2016, was cut from the same cloth. Hock has a high regard for the tough-tackling forward who, like him, also ended up at the Leigh Sports Village having established himself at Wigan and then joined Salford.

Frank Endacott, Stuart Raper and Mike Gregory all got positive on-field rewards from Hock.

Widnes coach Denis Betts got exactly that too when he took charge of a player that many predicted would be a handful for a year when the move to Parramatta broke down.

By then, changes were taking place at Wigan. Young back-rower Liam Farrell was coming to the fore, and as first the Vikings and then Salford swooped, his hometown club appeared to be getting on fine without him.

The next big chief to take Hock under his wing was, of course, Marwan Koukash.

Hock was paraded at a hyped-up glitzy launch under the 'Welcome to Hell' banner.

'We have recruited some great experience with our international players,' coach Brian Noble told the 450 fans and corporate guests at the Salford City Stadium.

'We have also added some exceptional young talent from home and abroad and are adding these to some of our existing players who have performed admirably this season.

'I am really excited about the prospects for this season. It is going to be one hell of a ride.'

To many onlookers, Koukash was trying to buy success, but Hock knew Wigan style structures had to be in place if major honours were to come his way.

Noble was welcoming and quick to talk Hock up.

They got on well and there were other familiar faces among Salford's new boys. Aussie scrum-half Tim Smith, for example, who had played with Hock at Wigan and against him with the Aussie Schoolboys. Smith knew Hock's game well, along with his many strengths and admired his power play down the middle.

And the respect was mutual, Hock telling reporters that: '...Timmy is a good bloke and a clever player.' The two got on well and had a great on-field understanding, as Hock also did with Michael Dobson.

With Sean Long on the Salford coaching staff, the situation seemed ripe for Hock to nail it.

Before the season was barely underway, no less a figure than Bobbie Goulding went on record saying he was playing like a true Man of Steel.

But once again internal change proved a distraction and disruptive influence.

Hock was caught up in this.

As we have read, he could never hit it off with Noble's eventual replacement, Iestyn Harris, for one thing and soon it was time for a third ruling chief to come into Hock's life when he packed his bags and left Salford for the final time.

Enter Derek Beaumont, the man who is intent on leading Leigh Centurions back into Super League.

A fresh start:
Hock has settled
in well at Leigh .

A nervous Hock sat alongside the outspoken Derek in the press conference that announced his signing for the Centurions at the start of 2015.

Leigh coach Paul Rowley told the press that the signing was not a gamble.

'I'm not concerned,' he said. 'We will be supportive and provide a stable environment. I am sure Gareth will fit in perfectly well. He's here as a rugby league player. The important thing is that he wants to be here.

'One thing you cannot doubt is that he is a fantastic rugby player. He's an imposing figure who will bring skill and aggression.

'He's a winner and we want winners at this club.'

It was chairman Beaumont, though, who set the agenda and let his own feelings and intentions be known.

He talked of a clean slate for Hock and said previous problems were a thing of the past.

He would judge Hock on how he found him not what people had said in passing conversation.

This was music to Hock's ears.

First-hand proof of a red carpet welcome, strong vision and a key role for the star signing in what was a family club.

Beaumont is protective of all his players and showed the watching media that Hock was very much wanted.

He spoke with the same level of passion and excitement as Maurice Lindsay had done all those years ago when a raw boned teenager was running hot for the town team.

Leigh coach Rowley considers Hock an international star and many in the game echo these sentiments.

Beaumont is honest and forthright. He has often spoken up for Hock, calling for Championship referees to give him a fair crack of the whip.

'Stop picking on Hock' was a recent headline in the *Manchester Evening News* that Hock read with interest, though the man himself was wary of being seen as making excuses.

'I knew exactly where Derek was coming from, but you just have to keep going,' was his take on it.

'It is frustrating at times and I guess I'm an easy target because of my reputation.'

Beaumont has revealed how time has been spent with Hock making sure he bought into the concept of keeping his cool on the field and not being intimidated by the opposition and their tactics.

The ever supportive Leigh boss reports a positive response and admires the way that Hock – by and large – refused to rise to the bait in 2015.

Such control has also pleased Paul Rowley. The duo claim the often volatile Hock is finally in a good place.

Maurice Lindsay thought he was all those years ago, but knew he too had to keep a look-out.

Lindsay did so much good for Wigan but could only do so much for Hock.

Speak to him now and Maurice stands by the view that Hock could easily have done what Burgess and Graham are currently doing in union and the NRL respectively.

Hock knew he had many strings to his talented bow but all too often, the wrong notes meant frustration for all concerned.

Brian Foley is another who can reflect on what might have been. Add Marwan Koukash to the list.

But maybe it could be third time lucky for Hock's latest keeper, Derek Beaumont.

Leigh pushed the boat out for Hock.

The fans have taken to him and so far it looks to have been a good move – a perfect fit.

Hock is still busy doing what he has always done best.

Players come and players go, but fans will certainly remember Gareth Hock.

For Maurice Lindsay, he was a gem to be reluctantly filed away under '...what might have been.'

Salford too felt they never saw the best of him.

Leigh chairman Beaumont is just pleased to see a happy Hock and is convinced the big fellow still has more impact to have on a sport where he could have been a king.

Three charismatic leaders then – all with an interesting tale to tell about one of the modern game's most talked about stars.

*Quite a handful:
Hock in action
at Leeds in 2007*

A time for tributes...

14

Wigan Warriors legend Andrew Farrell talks openly of Gareth Hock's consistent ability to pull something out of the bag.

Farrell rates Hock very highly – up with the best.

Faz also fondly remembers how Terry Newton became a father figure for the tough as teak back-rower.

A very gifted and bright all round footballer is Farrell's glowing labelling of Hock.

'You always wanted Gaz in your side,' says Farrell.

'You also always knew that the opposition hated playing against him.

'He is a top player with everything and he offered so much.'

Sean Long and Martin Gleeson freely admit they hated opposing Hock.

Long says: 'Hock was horrible to play against but what a fantastic player. He is incredibly tough and fearless. You always seemed to hit something hard when you tackled him.

'You absolutely knew about it. There was no escape.

'A truly fantastic player, so direct, so powerful and he should have won far more international honours.'

Martin Gleeson adds: 'Yes, an absolute nightmare to play against, such is his power, size and aggression.

'When happy and fit, he is the most destructive backrower in the game.

'He has a wonderful offload, he can win games and a centre thrives from being alongside such a powerful player.

'I put him up there with the best and know what he's capable of.'

Coach Brian Noble speaks equally highly of Hock.

He says: 'Players of Hock's stature and power do not come along that often.

'He would always be in my team – one of the first names on the sheet.

'I regard him as one of the world's best and finest back-rowers on his day.

'So direct and so uncompromising, yet a good guy. I have always thought a lot of him and know how he has to be coached and treated.'

Hock has a heart of gold according to his Leigh Centurion's teammate Ryan Brierley.

'A truly great player and an equally great bloke,' says Brierley.

'I've always admired him and it's only when you play with him you realise how good he is on and off the field.'

Aussie Tim Smith agrees with Brierley. He says: 'Gaz is a friend for life and what a player he is.

'He is so loyal and trustworthy.

'Aggressive on the field, somewhat shy off it. When on, as good as anyone in the game. Genuine class and an absolute competitor.

'We immediately hit it off – we could talk about anything. Hock is the complete player in my view.'

Bobbie Goulding pitches in: 'I've always rated Gaz very highly. I've always tried to look after him. He's a great lad and he's still mixing it with the big boys.

'He has everything and more in his make-up.'

As we've seen, Bill Ashurst saw Hock come up through the junior ranks and immediately knew Wigan had a huge star on their hands. So did Jackie Edwards – father of Wigan legend and current Wales RU coach Shaun – along with many others with a proven eye for top class home grown talent.

Andy Farrell says he always knew he could rely on Hock and also knew what it meant to him being a Wigan player.

Mick Cassidy saw the same and remembers a young Hock coming in for him and making his senior debut.

Cassidy is quick to acknowledge Hock's powerful style, his aggressive manner and formidable on-field presence.

Denis Betts waxed lyrical about Hock ahead of his highly-publicised move to Salford. Denis had seen Hock at his best for Widnes and could fully understand why Salford flashed the cash at the start of the Koukash era.

Speaking at the time, Betts said: 'Everyone knows just how good Hock is and what he is capable of.

'He can mix it with the best. Not only is he powerful, he is also gifted and skilful.

'Any team wants a Gaz Hock in it. He brings so much and he can impact on any game.'

Paul Rowley, Hock's current coach at Leigh, says: 'When I see Gaz smiling and happy, it makes me feel happy as his coach. It tells me that he is genuinely content and in a good place and enjoying training and playing.

'He has been smiling a lot since he came to Leigh and that's good. He is a big character and he is influential within the group.

'His talent was never in doubt and, in my view, he is still an international forward with so much to offer.'

Former Wigan hooker Wayne Goodwin, who announced his retirement at the end of the 2015 campaign, says: 'Gaz is certainly a tough guy who always rips into his rugby.

'You can never take the aggression out of him. He's always niggling, he's always in your face.

'I rate him highly and know for a fact you have to put your body on the line to try and stop him. He is a quality forward.'

Most players who played alongside Hock at Wigan echo Godwin's sentiments.

Josh Charnley talks up Hock's powerful running.

Micky McIllorum salutes Hock's steely characteristics and loved being in the same pack.

There is mutual respect with the likes of skipper Sean O'Loughlin, Kris Radlinski and so many others who have worn the cherry and white.

Sky Sports pundit Terry O'Connor, who packed down alongside Hock, says: 'Gaz is a great player – he had the ability to destroy teams. You always wanted him in the trenches with you.

'I remember one punch-up against Hull involving Gaz at a very early age. He was fearless and it kicked off when he moved from the back of the scrum and unleashed an uppercut on an opponent.

'I looked at him and you would've thought butter

wouldn't melt in his mouth but here he was, one hard player, truly world class and he did it against the best.

They couldn't contain him – I think the world of him.'

Micky Higham offers an interesting view on Hock. He says: 'Until you get to know the real Gareth Hock, you should not judge him or pass comment.

'He really is a great guy and a wonderful family man.

'He is one of the most talented players I have ever played with.

'He is a great friend with a great rugby brain and so much ability and power.

'I spent six weeks with him in Australia during the 2008 World Cup. I packed his bags when we moved from Sydney to Melbourne and further afield.

'I ran him a bath every single night to ease his aching back. I was like his valet, but I enjoyed it and I'd do it all over again. You always want to play with him, not against him.

'You only realise what he brings to a team when he's out there with you in the heat of battle.'

Hock's old adversary, Warrington's Ben Westwood, says: 'We became good friends at that World Cup and Gaz is a great player and a lad who will give you anything.

'I know I can always pick up the phone and have a chat and a laugh with him.

'It may have been months since we last spoke but he never changes – he's genuine and you never like playing against him.

'I can honestly say he is high up there among the toughest players I have ever played with.'

St Helens legend Paul Sculthorpe is fully supportive of Ben Westwood's testimonial for Hock.

He says: 'I remember this tall, rangy kid coming to the fore and through the ranks at Wigan.

'He had all the necessary assets. He was quick and he handled brilliantly.

'Gaz is a player I've always respected and rated highly.

'We were always wary of the threat he posed when playing for Wigan against Saints.

'A top quality forward with a tough side.'

Wigan's overseas stars have always been quick to talk Hock up.

They admire his fearless style.

Fuifui Moimoi, now in the front row at Leigh, says: 'I was very disappointed when Gaz did not come and play at Parramatta. His game is ideally suited for the NRL and I'm sure he would have had a massive impact in Australia.

'It is now an honour to be in the same team as him at Leigh. I have played against him at international level and know what a fierce competitor he is. He is incredibly brave and a forward who never lets anyone down.'

Sam Tomkins is among many high-profile players who say it is far better to be on the same side as Hock.

The writer of our foreword, Adrian Morley, agrees with Tomkins, reminding us that: 'It was Terry Newton who told me to look out for this lad Hock who was coming to the fore around 2006.

'Terry said he reminded him so much of me. He's a great player who is incredibly aggressive and effective. He is what I term an all-out rugby man and a born winner.'

Morley enjoyed packing down alongside Hock at Salford.

So too did Reds star in 2015 Scott Taylor, who says: 'Gaz is a true competitor. It was a pleasure to play with him at Salford. He's an incredible forward.'

Tommy Lee says: 'Hock's aggression and strength is incredible and he is one of those guys who's always there for you, wanting to help. I have total respect for him in all things.'

Junior Sa'u adds: 'There really is a great deal of good in Gaz. He is a top player. To be in the same side as him was an absolute pleasure.'

Salford talisman Rangi Chase enjoyed playing with Hock for club and country.

He says: 'We instantly hit it off like a house on fire. Hock has everything in his game and more.

'He's a truly great guy off the field, totally loyal and it's true, he would help anyone and be there for you. I rate him highly. He's one of the best – the tops.'

Super League's real hard men, such as Jamie Peacock and Malcolm Alker, have always relished battles with Hock, and no wonder given his brother-in-law Kevin Brown's description of him as being '...scared of no one. He has no fear in his body and has never ever taken a backward step.

'He never will.

'He is one of the toughest men I have ever met, yet he is so gifted and skilful.

'He has amazed me and is very misinterpreted.

'Off the field, he is one of the nicest guys you could ever come across. He has a heart of gold yet his life and his career has been like a soap opera.

'We leave the last word to Gareth's partner, Danielle, who sums him up thus: 'Gareth definitely is a strong and wonderful partner.

'He is also a very strong family man.

'If he only had a pound left in his pocket, he would part with it – that's my Gareth for you.'

My boyhood hero:
Andrew Farrell
was number one

My dream team...

15

After all those kind words about me, it's time I gave a bit of praise back and picked my rugby league dream team.

From being a kid, I only ever wanted to do one thing – play rugby league and play it for Wigan.

I've been fortunate enough to do both of those things, and have competed with and against some of the greatest rugby players on the planet.

One of them was my ultimate hero – Andrew Farrell, he had everything and more.

To be in the same team, to be in the same dressing room as Faz was an absolute thrill and a privilege.

Selecting a dream team was not easy.

Faz's name was the first on the sheet, he is joined by 12 other world class players.

I not only respect but admire and have the honour of

being with them in the heat of battle for club and country. So anyway, here is Gareth Hock's Dream Team:

FullBack

Sam Tomkins: Sam is the best fullback in the world in my book – which this is! We came up through the ranks together and he is one class act.

He is a good lad and we have known one another since we were kids. We have enjoyed holidays in Marbella and what a good player he is.

Sam's rugby brain is razor sharp. He can read a game and is a match-winner.

He is a real good lad and I am so glad he's coming back to Wigan in 2016.

Wingers

Josh Charnley: So strong and we've had many a laugh together. We've enjoyed fishing trips and we have roomed together with England.

Josh is the complete finisher and he has no edge to him at all. His record is incredible.

He is a good player, strong, very direct and is everything you look for in a winger. He is also extremely tough and ultra-competitive.

Pat Richards: We got on from day one.

Pat was great for the dressing room. He's a good laugh but is also a great professional in everything that he does.

A points machine and a big-match player.

Very skilful and fast for such a big man. So relaxed but

totally focussed and he could win a game at the drop of a hat. He's a sensational goal-kicker and running back too.

Centres

Martin Gleeson: One of the best players of the modern era by a country mile. Such good feet and so much talent.

He could make and score tries from anywhere. Add to this a great off-load and you have one classy centre.

He's a top lad off the field, too. I've so much time for him. He had everything in his locker and was the man for the big occasion at the highest level.

Kallum Watkins: A very good all round athlete who greatly impressed me from our time together with the England team.

He's a nice lad and he's very quiet, but he's one of the best in Super League and he's heading for the top.

He is strong, he has deceptive pace and has everything you look for in the make-up and build of a top class centre.

I like Kallum a lot.

Stand-off

Trent Barrett: Absolutely mad when he had a drink in him but moves ahead of the chasing pack.

One very big six who was brave, gifted and so strong.

A wonderful bloke off the field, strong in the tackle and the ability to unlock the tightest defence. Truly world class.

Scrum-half

Thomas Leuluai: Typically friendly Kiwi who would do anything for anyone. A real gent and a world class big-hitter.

We were quite close and for a little fella he was incredibly tough. His speed of thought is incredible and he is one of the cleverest players I have ever seen.

Prop forwards

Adrian Morley: Moz has the biggest biceps I have ever seen – they are bigger than Popeye's – as tough as they come.

A great friend of mine and Terry Newton's who runs and tackles hard every time. Hard but fair and a guy I've always looked up to and greatly admired.

Respected and feared by the Aussies, a truly fierce competitor.

Terry O'Connor: A very funny bloke, but come game time he ripped into anyone and everything.

One very good professional. I always appreciated the way he looked after the young lads, offering advice and encouraging us.

He was like a father figure and you won't find a more hard-working prop. I always got on with him and liked the way he played the game.

Hooker(s)

Micky McIllorum and Terry Newton: How do you choose between them? Impossible! They'd have to be on rotation.

I loved playing with Micky Mac. We pumped each other up. He's one of the best in the world and is a very dry lad. He is fearless and is a very good friend.

He always puts his body on the line and, like Adrian Morley, is as tough as they come.

As for Terry Newton, he was so skilful, he helped me

so much throughout my career. I modelled my game on Terry. I can't think of two finer and more aggressive hookers than this pair – true legends.

Second-rowers

Bryan Fletcher: Another big team player and a typical strong Aussie. Extremely skilful and a true leader who showed youngsters the way.

We had some good times together.

He was powerful and highly effective in the loose and had a presence about him and a good reputation.

Andrew Farrell: My childhood hero – the player I always wanted to be.

One of the fittest forwards I have ever seen and the best captain I ever played under.

Faz's toughness was unbelievable, a born leader and a true Wigan legend.

I can't think of a finer ball handling forward with such power and mental toughness.

Loose forward

Sean O'Loughlin: Some of the stuff Lockers does amazes me and he rarely makes a mistake.

I have known him since we were kids. We trained together, we played for Lancashire and England schoolboys.

There's no edge to him, a great lad and an equally great player. He instantly commands respect and leads by example in everything he does.

Here's to the next time...

16

Well, here we are at the close of 2015 and Leigh failed in its bid to get back into Super League. Our Middle 8 campaign was a disaster; it all went badly wrong, fuck knows why. Talk about being pissed off – that's an understatement. It just didn't happen and we were hurting at the end of it.

To be really successful in this game and to win the big matches when it really matters you need a strong winning desire throughout the team. I can honestly say that, in my view, not everyone had that in their make-up.

I was bitterly disappointed with my own performances. I could have done so much better. I really did feel we were more than good enough to go all the way because we had been strong in the regular season.

Yet we ended up winning just one game in our last seven. That was nowhere near good enough, unacceptable in fact and hopefully lessons have been learned. But we will go again and be better equipped. We kicked off the Middle 8 at home to Hull KR and led 24-6, but for some unknown reason we just didn't have it in us to close this and other games out. Rovers were there for the taking. When you build up such a good lead, you box it off. The need to do this was hammered home to me as a kid at Wigan. It was expected of you. I could see a few of the Leigh lads had switched off and that was frustrating, though they did give their all.

Rovers finished top but we were running them ragged. Had we won this game, I'm convinced we would've kicked on. We only had ourselves to blame for letting it slip.

Defeat was a big body blow and I was in the wars. I've had a few problems with my knee over the years and with 20 minutes to go against Rovers I was in trouble. I jumped and twisted awkwardly and knew straight away something was not right. I was gutted and needed surgery. To be ruled out of the second game back at Salford was sickening. If ever there was a game I wanted to play in it was that one. Instead, I ended up going under the knife.

When we got done by Salford we had it all on to be in the promotion mix after two defeats. Too many things were going against us as a club.

I had surgery to repair a torn cartilage and was told I'd be sidelined for eight weeks – I couldn't believe it. I was back inside three because I felt I owed it to Leigh to be out there busting a gut to get us into Super League. I wanted to do it for Derek Beaumont, who has been magnificently supportive of me and my family since we arrived.

I had always had and enjoyed a belting working relationship with Maurice Lindsay at Wigan and it's the same with Derek. They understand me and, as I have said before, Derek immediately made me feel wanted and part of Leigh.

If anyone can do whatever it takes to get us up it is Derek. He is a fan and knows the game. He cares enormously for his players and everyone else associated with the club – like Maurice, he's strong, determined and a leader.

I was never overly close with Marwan Koukash at Salford and the current Wigan owner Ian Lenagan is very different from Maurice. Lenagan keeps himself to himself and runs Wigan like a business. We didn't speak too much.

I speak regularly with Derek whose interest and support is genuine. He will offer advice, you can text him and he'll get back to you. To be able to chat to him is good. His passion for Leigh is incredible, it seems to get stronger and he continues to be an enormous help. I really do want to see the club back in Super League for his sake. It's just waiting to happen. The coaching staff are great too and there are so many other good people inside the club such as Alan Rowley, Mike Latham and Jane, the girl who does the wages. They're a great crowd and everyone is in it together but I guess we let ourselves down when it mattered most.

I came back from injury too early and was nowhere near right. I actually told Paul I was nowhere near fit, but he asked me to give it a go. I had to, yet I pulled out of the Sheffield game after we had trained on the Saturday morning. I knew I couldn't do myself justice in the game and was struggling.

I then returned against Halifax and this was an absolute shocker; we didn't turn up and we were beaten easily. I could hardly walk, let alone run, come the closing stages. I was out there far too long and possibly did myself more harm than good battling on. I agreed to have two pain-killing injections in my knee just to try and get me through games. I was way below par and the knee is still giving me a bit of jip.

I really was worried at first wondering what the full

extent of the damage was and I needed a good long rest before returning to pre-season training. I couldn't train in the week during the Middle 8s, I had to chance it during the matches.

We also lost at home to Wakefield, another game we could and should have won, but we failed to turn the screw and press home our advantages. You would've thought the penny would've dropped by now about letting teams off the hook but, having said that, so many teams were raising their game against us and playing out of their skin.

Opponents seemed to hate us and clearly wanted our scalp. Referees were giving us fuck all and don't forget the club didn't get a penny from the televised home games. This was a joke and we had no luck from the start. The fifty-fifty calls were going against us and we were possibly trying too hard at times. It was frustrating and we just couldn't serve up that bit extra that is the difference between winning and losing. I still find it hard to believe Rovers topped the group. They couldn't live with us in that first match.

The horror show I talked about at Halifax meant we had to beat Bradford at home to keep alive our promotion dream. I was again unable to train in the build-up and I told Rowls the team would be carrying me with me literally on one leg, but again he said he really needed me out there.

I feel that the way things worked out for Leigh in the Middle 8 really hurt Paul because expectation levels were so high. And I really felt for the fans. They are superb and Super League needs them.

Bradford beat us and we were fucked. We squared it at the break but again just couldn't get a win. I broke my nose early doors and there were some broken hearts and bodies at the finish. Derek rallied the players and the fans after the game like only he can. He said we dig in and go again in 2016.

I'm up for it, yet I talked of retiring when my time was up at Salford earlier in the year. Having now turned 32, I still feel good and am ready for another shot at the big prize. I was playing so well until my knee went.

We signed off our campaign at Widnes. The referee was awful. He was on my case and in my ear from the kick-off. We led, were smashing Widnes, but then we let in 50 points and that was that. I was sin-binned for a challenge on Rhys Hanbury. Yes it was high, but I've seen worse, far worse in fact, but the man in the middle couldn't resist pulling out a card and off I went. It was the third time in the season this particular fella had ordered me off, too much of a coincidence if you ask me.

Season over then and the annual Mad Monday piss up was spent on the ale in Liverpool. Not a bad day, but I ended up losing my phone and all my contact numbers. Tom Spencer and Jamie Acton arrived for the party dressed as gladiators. We told them it was fancy dress and they fell for it – boy did we laugh when they rolled up.

I decided a good rest was needed and vital before getting back into the daily grind of pre-season training. I'm still very hungry to do my bit for Leigh.

Retirement talk surfaced at Salford because I was totally pissed off with the place, with how it was being run and how I was being treated. Signing for Leigh definitely saved my career and renewed my passion.

I then saw Derek's own passion and determination, hence my goal to give him something to shout about. I know what seeing Leigh back in Super League alongside Wigan would mean to him. He puts him money where his mouth is and he just never gives up. He is a hard man, a fighter, I see so many fine characteristics in him.

He has already made his and Leigh's future intentions

clear by bringing in Rangi Chase, Harrison Hansen and Cory Paterson from Salford, for 2016. Rene Matiua is also coming from the Red Devils. I've played against him too and he's a strong player. Rangi would boost any side with his skill. He really is a class act and we've always hit it off. Everyone knows what he's capable of and what he can do.

Fucking hell, if Leigh don't go up in 2016, it really is God help us, because we are so stronger and wiser. Our form did dip but games were still there to be won. We did mess up.

Me and Harrison go back a long way. He came through at Wigan and he is the ultimate professional who trains hard. I met up with him in Liverpool when we were on Mad Monday. The Salford lads were also out in some of the same city bars and we had a good chat. He will be a good signing and will add strength and experience.

Cory also brings vast experience. I rate him but it's that winning desire I've talked about that we need. You never ever give up in games.

Micky Higham was absolutely outstanding for us in the Middle 8. He ran his blood to water. He has a big heart and he certainly did everything he could to secure promotion. You have to have players like Micky. He's a class act, he never throws in the towel and never knows when he's beaten.

I then enjoyed a good rest in Cyprus with Danielle and the kids. I was best man at the wedding there of my good friend, Mark Roberts. A bit of sunshine was welcome; it has recharged the batteries. I have also spent time doing up the family home at Rainford. I love it where we have settled.

I love life at Leigh and have unfinished business. Leigh fans did not see the real Gareth Hock at the end of the season. They watched a player who was struggling and there's nothing worse than knowing you are not 100 per cent right in the big games. You are helpless – absolutely helpless.

I really had lost the will to play at Salford and this is why I was low, but I am now in a good place and to take Leigh into Super League would rank highly among my on-field achievements. There is plenty to look forward to.

Looking back over my career as a whole has been enjoyable. Maybe I did not fulfil my potential, but I've no regrets and know I've given everything every time I've put on a pair of boots. I will do so as long as I am playing. The hunger and the desire are still there and I firmly believe the bright lights of Super League will shine on Leigh sooner rather than later. We won't fall short a second time – disappointment fuels desire.

As we come to the end of my tale – for now! – my mind goes back to when I was banned for taking drugs as a young lad, just starting out at Wigan. Shaun Wane came to our house on the day of the test results, having been in the same class as my mum at school. He knew our family and he knew me better than anyone. He also knew that I had ballsed up good style, but stayed remarkably supportive. He stood by me and he told me to keep my chin up, speaking like only he can.

From time to time, I still wonder whether I was right to turn down Parramatta. But then I look at Heidi, our beautiful and delightful blonde toddler, who is into everything and the apple of her doting daddy's eye.

She loves to blow kisses and is the reason I now know that kissing goodbye to a dream NRL move was the right thing to do. I enjoyed playing in Australia, but I always used to get homesick. I like being close to home and with the family. I am a home boy at heart.

When I proposed to Danielle early in 2015, she thought we were just going for a new car. We got to Preston Audi and Neil, the boss there, made it a real celebration. A message from me came up on the big screen in the showroom asking

Danielle: 'Will you marry me?' She said yes and ended up with more than a new Audi Q5. It was one of the best days of my life. We sipped champagne and laughed about what they had done for us.

Along with controversy, laughs have always been a big part of my career, such as the time the Wigan lads sent me to a Chinese restaurant with an order for 'fried rice and minge'. Guess what? They were out of it that day! Kev Brown was behind that one and he still reminds me about it.

Hopefully there will be plenty more to smile about as my playing days wind down.

I asked Neil Barker if he would write my book because we've always got on and been able to talk. He is probably the only rugby reporter I've ever got on with and trusted. I have greatly enjoyed charting my journey with him and have been brutally honest with what I've said and what I've offered an opinion on.

Yes, I've made mistakes and plenty of them, but I've always remained strong and never given up.

I heeded Waney's advice.

To now give up on helping Leigh's Super League dream become reality would be wrong. I'll be back, mark my words, doing again what I love doing. We are going to dig in, like Derek says.

I guess I'll keep the referees busy and will continue to get under some people's skin, but my love for rugby league is as strong as the day I set out on this journey.

And right now, the real Gareth Hock still has a pair of boots to lace up. Who knows what the next few years have in store – let's just wait and see.

One thing is for sure: I have no regrets.

My career stats

To September 2015

International

Test Matches – By Team

Team	Years	App	T	G	DG	Pts
Great Britain	2006	4	0	0	0	0
England	2008-09, 2012	5	0	0	0	0
Total	2006-2012	9	0	0	0	0

International Matches – By Team

Team	Years	App	T	G	FG	Pts
England	2003, 2008, 2012	5	3	0	0	12
Total	2003-2012	5	3	0	0	12

World Cup Matches – By Team

Team	Years	App	T	G	FG	Pts
England	2008	3	0	0	0	0
Total	2008	3	0	0	0	0

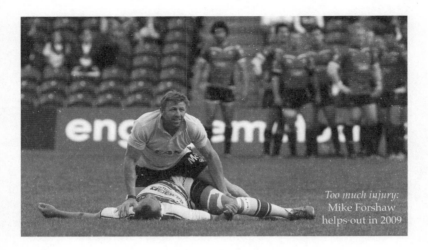

Too much injury: Mike Forshaw helps out in 2009

Domestic

English League Career - By Year

Team	Year	App	T	G	FG	Pts
Wigan	Challenge Cup - 2003	3	3	0	0	12
	Super League VIII - 2003	29	8	0	0	32
	Super League IX - 2004	30	2	0	0	8
	Challenge Cup - 2004	5	2	0	0	8
	Super League X - 2005	3	1	0	0	4
	Challenge Cup - 2006	1	0	0	0	0
	Super League XI - 2006	14	2	0	0	8
	Super League XII - 2007	27	1	0	0	4
	Challenge Cup - 2007	4	0	0	0	0
	Super League XIII - 2008	17	6	0	0	24
	Challenge Cup - 2008	2	0	0	0	0
	Super League XIV - 2009	15	4	0	0	16
	Challenge Cup - 2009	2	2	0	0	8
	Super League XVI - 2011	8	3	0	0	12
	Challenge Cup - 2011	1	0	0	0	0
	Super League XVII - 2012	26	11	0	0	44
	Challenge Cup - 2012	4	3	0	0	12
	Super League XVIII - 2013	0	0	0	0	0
Widnes	Super League XVIII - 2013	16	9	1	0	38
	Challenge Cup - 2013	1	1	0	0	4